Tapping Into Financial Freedom

Clear the Confusion and Promote Your Prosperity
Using Emotional Freedom Techniques

KATHERINE HACKING

Author: KathyHacking.com

Publisher: BeamPublishing.net

Dedication

Special thanks to Angela Gifford, Dee Jennings, and April Beam, for helping to bring this content into the shape of a book so that it can impact the world.

This book of applied Emotional Freedom Technique is for all the children who grew up confused about money and feeling ashamed or guilty for the financial hardship around them.

May the progress we choose to create inside ourselves generate beautifully sustainable outcomes that will bless our families.

Table of Contents

Introduction

Welcome, welcome. This is a 'Tapping with Kathy' series for recovery from financial abuse.

First, we're going to do a little bit of introduction to emotional freedom techniques, because that is the primary tool that we will be using throughout our time together.

The EFT tapping approach that many people in the United States know and use today was developed by engineer Gary Craig in the 1990s. His method was largely inspired by the work of clinical psychologist Roger Callahan, PhD.

Emotional Freedom Techniques is a mind-body therapy that draws on the traditional Chinese medicine (TCM) practice of acupuncture, and it is used today as a self-help approach in modern psychology. Standard EFT tapping typically incorporates nine acupressure points (acupoints) on the face, hands, and body.

We will be gently tapping key acupoints with our fingertips while focusing on uncomfortable feelings or concerns to release the stuck emotions, and then using positive affirmations to embed new frequencies and thought patterns for the mind/body system to learn new ways of being.

Research of EFT used in clinical settings suggests that tapping can relieve levels of stress, depression, and anxiety, diminish cravings, improve performance, and even help relieve symptoms of post-traumatic stress disorder (PTSD).

You should know that there are meridian pathways that move energy throughout your body. And on each of the meridians, there are acupressure points that we will be stimulating with touch.

One of the things I most often forget that you might want to do, is to assess and track your level of distress before you begin. That means anytime you sit down to tap, you might take out a piece of paper and first write down what it is that's bothering you and how much it bothers you.

Measure that distress level zero to ten. How big is it? A five or six, would be "I'm still functional, but I'm not really happy." Versus the 9 or 10 - "I'm on the edge! I'm not functional and I can't carry on anymore!"

Then as you tap, that's the thing that you're going to check in on again; what is your number, "subjective units of discomfort or displeasure" (SUDS) level now? And where I usually forget to do that at the beginning, I can't specifically go look at my own number and say, "Oh, it was an 8, now it's a 3." I just know internally that it is improving.

You will also want to pay attention to your low-level irritations. If you're tapping for something and it's improving, (awesome, keep going!) Don't just bring it down to a bearable 1 or 2 and then walk away. Keep going a couple more rounds and get the little tail ends and quiet background noise bits of thought cleaned up too so that that topic is more completely cleared.

In over 20 years of tapping, I have never had exactly the same problem surface again. But frequently there are aspects of it that if I had stayed a tiny bit longer with the tapping, I could have gotten to and cleared that too. Instead, I waited for it to become an obvious irritation again before I stopped attending to those bits later. Okay?

Give maybe 3 more minutes with each session. Go beyond where you can breathe easier and reach for the euphoria of popping your belief system bubbles. It could bring you massive progress very quickly.

The SUDS level movement is your primary way to track your progress. Assessment of your subjective units of displeasure or discomfort can be done at the beginning and end of each round, zero to 10, before moving on to another topic.

The set-up phrase is adapted for each topic. The words spoken while you are tapping gently on the side of the hand (at the karate chop point) can even incorporate the SUDS level.

Remember to keep tapping while speaking out loud some combination of "Even though I have (this irritation/this SUDS level) going on, I accept myself."

You will need to repeat the set-up phrase 3x's to be very clear with your system what you are targeting with your rounds of tapping.

Begin again with the setup phrase any time you get distracted or interrupted. If you are continuing the same subject, you won't need to redo the set-up portion for additional rounds.

Tapping has been shown to relieve emotional, mental, and physical stress and positively impact gene expression in the body. So, whether you want to heal your spirit and heart, your body and mind, your relationships, your finances, or something else, you can benefit from Meridian Tapping.

The Basic Emotional Freedom Techniques Recipe

Here are the main points to tap on:

1. EB = Eyebrow point-, at the beginning of the eyebrow, above the nose.

2. SE = Side of the Eye, on the bone bordering the outside of the eye.

3. UE = Under the Eye, on the cheek bone directly under the eye.

4. UN = Under Nose, in the center of the area between the nose and top lip.

5. CH = Chin, in the center between the bottom lip and bottom of the chin.

6. CB = Collarbone, right under your collarbone, about 3 inches to the left or right from the midline at the clavicular notch.

7. UA = Under the Arm, on the side of the body about 4 inches below the armpit.

8. LP = Liver Point, 2" under your breast on the right side (or both sides)

9. WR = Bump your wrists together, where your hand bends to meet the arm.

10. TH = Top of the head. A large area toward the back of your crown.

The Energy Points

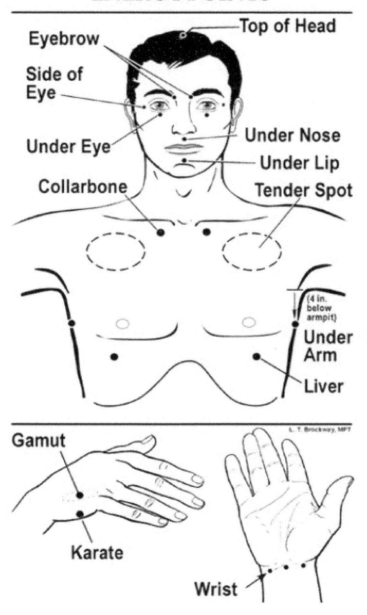

Other Points

KC = Karate Chop point. The soft pad on the side of the hand at the base of both little fingers (used for Reversals or as the set-up point.

The Gamut point. On the back of the hand, in the soft tissue between the pinky and ring fingers.

The Tender or sore spot. Shown as a large area in the soft tissue, below the clavicle on both sides of the sternum. The set-up phrase was initially taught by rubbing the tender/sore spot, on either or both sides, in a circular motion with two or three fingers.

The Finger points (not shown on diagram) are found at the base of each fingernail bed on the side closest to the thumb. These acupoints on each finger are very helpful for tapping discreetly in the moment of an upsetting situation - when you cannot step away to the privacy of another room or visit the bathroom to tap without an audience.

The acupoints on the fingers are frequently omitted because they are also stimulated when we use our fingers to tap the other points or fidget by drumming our fingers on the table.

What follows is a dynamic and blended application of EFT for financial topics supported by extensive training in many healing modalities.

I deeply appreciate the educational content created by so many authors and teachers such as Richard Bach, Jane Roberts, Gary Frese, Wayne Dyer, Deepak Chopra, Esther Hicks, Tony Robbins, Caroline Myss, Gary Craig, Joe Vitale, Jessica Ortner, Dain Heer, Gary Douglas, Jarrad Hewett, Matt Kahn, Brene Brown, Joe Dispenza, Megan

Sillito, and hundreds of others! They have facilitated and inspired my growth and healing over the past 20 years.

The journey to recover my own wholeness has not been easy and I do not yet claim completion; but I count myself lucky to have found Gary Craig and his Emotional Freedom Techniques in 2005.

EFT holds a special place in my heart as it was the first modality that let me help myself work through nightmares and panic attacks. It is tapping that first let me move beyond my own arachnophobia and fears about public speaking.

My certifications with EFT gave me the gift of self-reliance and the necessary tools to bring myself through many physical, emotional and financial challenges as a mom, artist, practitioner and teacher.

This book is specifically for clearing financial topics, but I want to be very clear in saying that Emotional Freedom Techniques is an adaptable tool that can assist you through any challenge. The tagline for tapping is 'Try it on anything!' and I hope you will learn to use it that way.

Getting Started with Meridian Tapping

Our topic right now is all the current financial mess and shared money stress. A beginning set up phrase could be "I deeply and completely accept myself, even though I have all of this financial stress right now." Okay?

That's a baseline. You begin with tapping on the side of the hand and saying "Even though…" and you fill in the blank with what is true for you. "Even though I'm stressing right now about money, I choose to deeply and completely love and accept myself."

Another version of that, especially if you're working with children, would be "Even though I'm stressing about money, I know that my mother loves me, or I know that my family loves me."

Especially if it is difficult for someone to say, for themselves, of themselves, that they care for themselves, you can begin with, "I know that (a specific) someone cares for me, or I know that I am safe right now."

The set-up statement just needs 3 spoken repetitions. They can be varied, or the exact same words stated three times while tapping the karate chop point.

You will get more awareness of the energy moving through the meridians as you start to use this technique regularly. You do not need to learn about the meridians to be able to use this process. You do not ever need to feel what is happening as it is happening to benefit from Emotional Freedom Techniques.

Also, as you speak aloud while tapping through the points, listen for any verbal 'slip of the tongue' or internal mind chatter. Those are clues for you about related words, experiences, and emotions that are connected inside your personal 'mind map' for each topic.

So then, as we move to tap on the rest of the tapping points, you're going to use a short reminder phrase about your topic at each of the points. A good generic one to say here is "Stress about money."

You will tap using your first two fingers. 2 or 3 fingers is plenty. This is a gentle, moderate speed tapping. There should not be any lasting residual redness after you finish tapping on an area.

We're going up to the beginning of the eyebrow, at the inner edge by your nose. Either side works. You may tap both sides together, but you do not need to tap both sides. Say "Stressing about money." Then move to the side of the eye, and you say your reminder phrase again, "Stressing about money." Next, tapping under the eye just softly, on the cheekbone below the pupil. Yep, say out loud, "Stressing about money. All this stress about money."

Tapping under the nose, just at the midline. Say "Stressing about money. Money stress. Yep, I've got it." On your chin, right under your lips, "Stressing about money." Remember to breathe as you tap through the points.

Then tapping on your collarbone. There are lots of points right there, so anywhere along your collarbone works, but we will aim for central, within about 2 inches either side at the clavicular notch. Say out loud "Oh, this stress about money and bills!" And you can hear, you can feel what that brings up in your body.

15

You can stick with saying "Stressing about money." Or as you'd like, change the words so that it brings up different related emotional textures.

Next, tapping under your arm about 3 - 5 inches below the armpit, on the midline on the side of your ribs (either side or both). Say "Stressing about money."

There is a point you can see on your diagram labeled Liver Point. It is found on your ribcage, a few finger widths below the end of the sternum and a few inches away from the midline, left and right on both sides - without leaving the front of the body. For women, it's where the band of your bra is usually falling.

The Liver Points can be socially awkward, so many people skip this point, but tapping on the ribcage at the Liver Point can be very relevant to shifting anger or resentment. Include this area whenever possible.

Tapping (or rubbing in a circle could be easier) on the Liver point, say "Stressing about money."

Next, the inner wrist points, "Stressing about money." Then move to tapping the crown of the head and say, "Stressing about money. All this stress about money."

We began tapping on the soft tissue at the pinky side of the hand, while repeating the set-up phrase three times and then continued tapping at the eyebrow point, moved down through the points in sequence and came back to end with the tapping on the crown. That was one round of EFT.

Take a breath and check in with yourself about your subjective units of discomfort. What was your SUDS number at the beginning? What is your SUDS level now?

Did your SUDS level change with just one round? Just notice. Maybe make a note if you are logging your topics and personal progress. Did you find a slightly different wording of your topic that feels more urgent or relevant to address? Okay, that's just one round of tapping.

Now, on the basic recipe reference (image A) you can see something next to the Karate Chop point called the Gamut Point. There is a soft spot on the back of your hand that is used for the Gamut Point Technique.

You only need to do the Gamut Point process if your SUDS number isn't changing; if you've tapped on your topic for a few rounds and it still seems the same. Instead of continuing to just tap and not feel like you're getting anywhere, use The Gamut Point Technique.

This is a way of adjusting your polarity and rebalancing your brain so that you can be here now. Then, when you do more rounds of tapping again, with your full system oriented to the present moment you will have an easier time shifting and changing.

If someone says, "[This] has been my problem my whole life. I can't change it with anything!" Start with the Gamut Point Technique for orientation purposes. It will balance the hemispheres of the brain so that the individual is fully present to benefit in a bilaterally synchronized way.

The Gamut Point Technique – "9 Point Gamut"

You only need to do this part of the sequence if an issue seems to be stuck. It balances the right and left hemispheres of the brain. Locate the gamut point on the back of your hand. It is in the soft tissue between the little finger and ring finger knuckles and down about an inch.

Continue gently tapping on that spot while repeating a reminder phrase and doing the following sequence:

1. & 2. Close your eyes tightly, then open them wide (remember to keep tapping and saying the reminder phrase during the whole gamut point process)

3. & 4. While keeping your head straight & still, using your eyes only, look down as far as possible to the right, then down & as far as possible to the left.

5. & 6. Roll your eyes around in a big circle as if looking at all the numbers on a big clock. Roll your eyes around in the opposite direction (Keep tapping and saying the reminder statement).

7. Hum for 2 seconds a familiar song like "Happy Birthday" or "Jingle Bells" It does need to be a tune with words for this process to activate the correct part of your brain.

8. Count rapidly from 1 to 6 while moving your eyes to look from the floor to the ceiling.

9. Hum again for 2 seconds of the same song chosen in step seven.

Test Your Results.

Note: If you get stuck and are not getting the results you want, the reason may be:

1. You may have a Polarity or Psychological Reversal – try tapping on the karate chop point for your set up statement, saying emphatically or shouting "Even though, for some reason, I DON'T REALLY want to let go of (this issue)! I COMPLETELY ACCEPT MYSELF NOW" Sounds odd but using the KC with more emphasis in the set up can make the difference in bringing all aspects of yourself forward to shift the content. Notice any stray thoughts that pop up! There may be another topic that your body would like to clear out first, for example: "I am not safe (in general). I am unable to relax, rest and digest." before "It isn't safe to talk about money."

2. You may be dehydrated. Get some water. Meridian tapping is stimulating movement along the meridian pathways and adjusting the body's energy (electrical) system. Electricity is conducted by water, sugar, and salt (electrolytes). Drink some water, maybe have a meal or snack, and try EFT again. Dehydration is the most common cause of EFT appearing not to work.

3. You may be stating your issue in terms that are too general. Be more specific, i.e. Even though: "My father punished me for _____ when I was 6." "I hold anxiety about_____ in my chest." or "I'm mad at my brother for lying about _____."

4. You may also have sensitivity to a substance that's blocking your progress. You may need to see an EFT practitioner to figure out this one, unless you know what your sensitivity is - then go ahead & start tapping for that

topic (The experiences & the emotions around being sensitive to that substance) first.

EFT works about 90% of the time, far more than any other type of therapy. If you're having problems, it's most likely to be for "mechanical" reasons. So, ask for help when you need it. The process of meridian tapping is fairly simple, and the benefit of an outside perspective can be miraculous!

Yay! That's the basics of Emotional Freedom Techniques.

The trick now is to keep going and, as much as possible, remember to use it on everything.

I think that you are here with this book because you have had a glimmer of hope that you can alter the trajectory of your financial life.

Beyond assisting you to reach that accomplishment, I hope you will also realize your growing capacity to impact the livelihood of those in your community and embrace a larger vision for your success.

Harmonizing with a Substance

Now that you have the basics, we are going to begin with something a little unusual. It's a tapping protocol for putting your body in harmony with a substance.

For this example, we will use a silver coin. Yes, use real money - coins or bills of any denomination. If it's actual legal currency, use it. It is money of all types that we would like to harmonize with.

Okay, to guide you through this process, I'm referencing something developed by Stacey Vornbrock, M.S., LPC, called, "Clearing the Energy of a Substance."

You only need one hand for your tapping. So, hold the money in one hand and get your other one ready for tapping. Left or right is fine, alternate as you wish. The acupoints for meridian tapping are found on both sides of your body. The meridian pathways are mirrored, left and right inside each of us.

You're going to tune into the substance. You don't have to have it physically present but if you do, it could also be placed in front of you to look at while you tap and talk. You could hold the substance and tap the side of that hand.

First, 0 to 10, do you have a SUDS level come up just for holding or looking at this substance? Is there discomfort in your body?

Notice what your body has to tell you. Is there anxiety or tension in your breathing right now? You could make a note of those sensations.

21

Begin by tapping the side of your hand. Say out loud "Even though my body is not in harmony with [silver], I deeply and completely love and accept myself. I deeply and completely love and accept myself even though my body is not in harmony with silver." and the third time, "I deeply and completely love and accept myself, even though my body is not in harmony with silver."

Move to the beginning of the eyebrow, tapping gently and saying "All the muscles in my body are not in harmony with silver. The muscles of my body are not in harmony with silver." Tapping at the side of the eye, say "All the ligaments in my body are not in harmony with silver. My body is not in harmony with silver." Under the eye, tap and say, "All the tendons in my body are not in harmony with silver." Under the nose, "All the joints in my body are not in harmony with silver." The chin point, "All the bones in my body are not in harmony with silver. My bones are not in harmony with silver."

Collarbone points, tapping still. Say "All the cartilage in my body is not in harmony with silver. The cartilage in my body has not yet harmonized with silver." Under the arm, "All the tissues in my body are not in harmony with silver." and let's use this one, tap the inner wrists to each other or use the fingertips of one hand to tap the other wrist. Say "My body is not in harmony with silver." Some people do not use their liver points or wrist points and skip to the top of the head after the under-arm point.

Going to the crown center, tapping on top of the head works to stimulate a lot of pathways at once. Say "The nerves in my body are not in harmony with silver." Keep going for round 2.

22

Tapping at the beginning of the eyebrow again "All the nerves in my body, all the fascia in my body are not in harmony with silver." Then at the side of the eye say, "All the membranes in my body are not in harmony with silver." Breathe deeply.

Tapping under the eye, "My skin is not in harmony with silver." Under the nose, "My spine is not in harmony with silver." The chin point, "All the fibers in my body are not in harmony with silver." At the collarbone, "All the fluids in my body are not in harmony with silver." Under the arm, "All the organs in my body are not in harmony with silver." Wrist points, "My body does not yet harmonize with silver." Then return to the top of the head. "My heart is not in harmony with silver."

Round 3. Gently back to tapping at the inner edge of the eyebrow say, "The neural pathways of my brain are not in harmony with silver." Side of the eye, "My ears are not in harmony with silver." Under the eye, "My eyes are not in harmony with silver." Under the nose, "My nose and sense of smell are not in harmony with silver. My mouth and taste buds are not in harmony with silver." Tapping at the chin point, "My senses of taste and touch are not in harmony with silver."

Collarbone points, "My body doesn't know what to do with silver." Tapping under the arm, "My auric field is not in harmony with silver. All this stuff about silver; having it, not having it." Wrist points, tap and say, "Silver and I are not yet friends." And then tapping at the top of the head. "My energy body is not in harmony with silver, but my body is now learning about silver."

Now for this protocol we use the side of the hand, the karate chop point for another set up phrase series. Tapping the KC point, say out loud, "I give my body permission to fully and completely harmonize with [this substance] silver, even though all of this is new to me. My body can choose to relax and let go of any disharmony with silver. I can choose to let go and change this. I give every cell in my body permission to easily and comfortably harmonize with silver."

Let that topic rest for now. You might come back through to use this tapping sequence with other substances held in hand or in mind. An example might be $1, $5, $10, $20, $50 or $100 bills, copper, nickel, zinc, steel, ruby, pearl, emerald, sapphire, lapis, amethyst, diamond, gold or platinum.

Remember to breathe and recheck your SUDS level.

Interesting. Why do we go through the negative, the disharmony of a topic first? It is just like when we use a GPS. The system needs to know where you are to accurately begin the navigation to your destination.

It is the same with tapping. You want to start by tapping while you name what's wrong. Talk about what's been dysfunctioning as honestly as possible. What have you noticed that is uncomfortable around your topic? As we tap and talk through the negative thoughts and emotions, you get to hear what you think and what you are feeling. Which words have a zing to them? Pull on those threads as you keep tapping.

Acknowledge the foundation that needs to be addressed. Notice how your body stiffens or relaxes as you tap and speak out loud. Let your body show you where

24

your patterns have been holding energy in place. These are the patterns that are keeping your thoughts and actions looped into recreating the same problems for your future.

For example, some people find that they hold their breath and have tension in their jaw, neck, shoulders, lower back, hands, or legs when they know there's going to be a financial problem. Notice, what has been your habit? Where does your body hold tension? Maybe it is that you avoid looking. Do you not open the mail; not answer the phone? Do you not keep any of your receipts or records so you can pretend like you didn't spend the money?

You can use this book of tapping prompts to move the energy in your body around small and large problems. Start this journey to your Financial Freedom with tapping for the things that you can easily think of and the generic topics that many people share. Be sure to pause and address your specific experiences also.

A Commitment to Yourself

Most of us have a hard time talking about our monetary and financial beliefs. We have been taught to hide the experiences that shape our financial reality.

We know that there is conditioning through family, culture and religion telling us that these things (the personal details of money and finances) are very private, secret, or shameful to discuss.

While I am not advocating that you speak with everyone about everything; I am saying that traditional secrecy is a great burden for the people who are struggling to change their outcomes and improve the quality of life for themselves, their families, or communities.

The things that we collectively avoid discussing make great content for rounds of tapping with Emotional Freedom Techniques.

Are you willing to be different? Will you choose to have emotional freedom around everything connected to money? Will you give yourself the gift of emotional clarity and mental resourcefulness where other people trip on shame and fear?

What if you can tap your way into financial freedom and generate new outcomes for yourself?

Try voicing some of these common money worries and fears while tapping through the points. Feel free to change the wording at any point, so that it better fits your personal phrasing and vocabulary.

Any one of the following statements could be used with its own set up and full rounds of tapping through all of the points.

Tapping this way, called "daisy-chaining," we will hit many aspects around the general topics of Financial Abuse and Financial Freedom. This approach can show you where there are sore topics that need your attention to reduce the SUDS level further and allow your capacity to think clearly to come back online with ease.

Start with the clavicular sore spot or at the KC point at the side of the hand. Repeat out loud 3 x's - "Even though I have a lot of content coming up around the subject of money, I chose to focus on the possibility that things can change for the better."

EB - "I don't want to talk about this!" SE - "I feel ashamed about the state of my finances." UE - "Money is just complicated." UN - "I am so embarrassed about the state of my finances!" CH - "Thinking about money brings up fear; it brings up tension and anxiety." CB - "Even knowing that this tapping thing could be good for me, I don't want to do this." UA - "I know I don't want to remember all the painful details!" LP - "It is uncomfortable to feel these things!" WR - "There are good reasons why we don't talk about our money." TH - "It is better to just keep quiet and stay silent. At least that way I can look good occasionally."

Take a deep breath. Follow your breath all the way in and all the way out.

Tapping at the EB - "I've kept quiet about money for so long. I don't like all the secrets around money." SE - "I'm going to give myself some space here. I'm choosing honesty within myself, for myself right now." UE - "I am voicing these things right now for my own benefit." UN - I don't have to talk about these emotions with anyone else- unless I want to." CH - "Maybe I want to hear what I have to say. It might be good to admit to myself how I am feeling."

CB - "Maybe speaking things out loud is already helping my mind and body to release heavy and painful patterns about money." UA - "I don't even want to think about my money most of the time. I've been avoiding my financial details." LP - "It's hard to change something when I keep avoiding it." WR - "Something bad might happen if I open up about all of this. It might make someone mad." TH - "I'm worried. My life might change. I'm NOT SURE I really, really want my money to change."

Keep breathing and keep tapping. Repeat after me:

EB - "Is that true? Do I want my finances to stay the way they are right now?" SE - "What might happen if I could let go of my fear, even just a little bit?" UE - "What if I could start to feel less stress about money?" UN - "What if talking and tapping gently on acupoints actually does change something for me?" CH - "What might it be like to allow my life to flow with more money?"

CB - "Am I willing to embark on a new pathway?" UA - "Oh! My life could change in very enjoyable ways! Could I handle having things go well for me?" LP - "What would it be like to change my money reality?" WR - "I'd like to have new experiences around money. I am willing for my life to change too." TH - "I am open to the possibility that this tapping for emotional freedom could help me in many ways."

Take a deep breath in and blow it out.

I have worked with and trained under amazingly skilled and talented healing practitioners, ministers, shamans, massage therapists, oracles, and facilitators across the United States.

One common thread throughout my career with so many modalities is the understanding that each person, faced with very different layers of pain and dysfunction, will need to choose to heal.

The human mind is an amazingly powerful tool to work with and nearly impossible to work against.

As writer Richard Bach says, "Argue for your limitations, and sure enough they're yours."

So, I am going to ask you to choose. Will you now make a commitment to creating your financial future?

Will you take actions that open space to alter your own inner mapping? Will you follow this gentle pattern of tapping acupoints?

Will working through this content be a monthly or weekly, 'slow and steady progress' kind of project?

Could you make an appointment with yourself for 15 - 30 min of tapping once a week?

I hope you are saying "Yes, yes and YES!"

Welcome. It's time to tap into financial freedom!

Identifying Financial Abuse

What is financial abuse? There are actually a lot of pieces to this problem. You might want to tap along your collarbone or other acupoints while you read this section.

Learning about this, the definition of financial abuse, is what inspired the creation of the original live EFT for Financial Freedom series that I first taught in 2018.

Like other forms of abuse, the simple explanation of financial abuse is where one person takes advantage of another persons' financial vulnerability to benefit themselves.

Active financial abuse is a common tactic used by abusers to gain power and control in a relationship. It is often a component of a larger problem that includes other types of abuse, and it is frequently overlooked in the struggle to escape from and recover from the more physically damaging forms of abuse.

Financial abuse may be subtle or overt but in general, it will include tactics to conceal information, limit the victim's access to assets, or reduce accessibility to the family records i.e., keeping secret accounts, lying about the cost of expenses or the amount of donations to a political or religious group.

Financial abuse ranges from obvious deceit to complex manipulations. There is the confusion of being blamed and punished for someone else's financial problem, but this also includes anywhere you have been taught to blame other parties for your financial problems.

There are financially abusive circumstances of fraud perpetrated by individual con-artists, groups, corporations, and governments. The failure to disclose details, or direct misrepresentation of facts causing heartache and bankruptcy for our elderly population has become so common that we have TV shows about it!

As of 2021, estimates of elder financial abuse and fraud costs to older Americans range from $2.6 billion to $36.5 billion annually.

We have ongoing commercialization of a fast paced and high-ticket lifestyle that promotes purchase-now-pay-later as the standard 'American way.'

Alongside that narrative is the popular degradation of the very poor and homeless populations as being some combination of inherently lacking intelligence, drug addicted, drunk, psychotic, incompetent or lazy.

These things all work together to keep us in the cycle of being divided and impoverished. We are collectively isolated in our shared financial fear and doubts.

We have generationally not been asking questions, not talking about money, and not educating people (particularly young women) about their financial options.

We have been suffering financial abuse as a society and then passing that on to the next generation through our unconscious habits. That makes money into an unknown, unnamed, and then unidentified boogeyman versus possibly having the awareness to wonder about alternatives, seeking freedom for curiosity, financial education, and the vocabulary to grow with it.

When you've got curiosity and awareness you have choices. From there we can change anything!

What Financial Education?

Let's do a few rounds of tapping for the "lack of a financial education" piece. Deep breath.

Make a note of your SUDS level. What comes up here? Zero to ten, for "No one taught me how to properly manage money."

Speaking aloud, tapping the KC point on the side of the hand, "Even though my parents did not teach me how to be responsible. how to be engaged with money, how to be smart with money, how to use money, or how to be wise with money…. I know now that I can choose, and I do choose to accept myself."

Take a big breath. Still tapping the KC - "I accept myself, even though I was undereducated about money. Even though I was not educated about money, in fact, I was neglected in terms of monetary education! There are all these words, all these uncomfortable financial things I was not prepared for. Things I've been taught to avoid. But I choose now to love and accept myself. I do now have this option; I choose to love myself, even though I have been financially uneducated."

Deep breath, tapping through the points.

EB - "I am financially uneducated." SE - "I am unprepared for the challenges of my life." UE - "I have been financially neglected." UN - "I was taught to be afraid of money." On the CH - "I was taught to avoid money."

Participant: I almost said something else there. Mine was "I was taught to overspend!" Is that ok?

Kathy: We are on the topic of things we've been taught. It's easy to guess that we've been taught different patterns and habits. Yes. When you find that something crops up in your mind, different vocabulary, use your words!

Your words are so much more pertinent to moving the energy for you and detangling your money reality. Definitely! Say what it is that comes up as it arises. You don't have to stick closely to this script. I'm giving you ideas to find your relevant threads.

Tapping at the CB - "I've been taught to misuse my money! I've been taught to misapply my resources!" UA - "I was taught to mislabel and miscalculate my reserves." LP - "I've been taught to misidentify what money is and what money is for." WR - "Who's allowed to have it? And who is not allowed to have it?" TH - "I've been taught a lot of things. I don't know all of what I was shown and told about all of that money stuff... And that's the point!"

EB - "There's so much I don't know! That's human nature to not know everything." SE - "There's so much my family didn't know and probably more they didn't know they did not know about money!" UE - "I have all of these patterns. Patterns about money; about avoiding money, about having and not having money." UN - "So much money stuff." CH - "Money garbage."

Participant: I was gonna say "Money shit."

Kathy: Yeah, that too. Cussing with your tapping is perfectly acceptable.

CB - "So much bullshit, horse shit, chicken shit about money!" UA "I've been living in this world....

Nevermind! I've been suffering in this world full of crap about money!" LP - "I'm sick of this shit!" WR - "This is unbelievable. I can't believe I've gotten this far with so little education." TH - "I've been torturing myself with all of this misidentified junk around money."

We're going back to the EB - "So much junk." SE - "Too much clutter to sort through about money." UE - "My brain is full of things that don't work with money." UN - "I have a legacy of bankruptcy. Bankruptcy!?" CH - "Financial, mental, emotional, spiritual, and physical bankruptcy. Overdrawn. Over-extended."

CB - "They're all connected. You know? It's such a big mess." UA - "This financial mess. This monetary mess." LP - "It's ridiculous that we live with so much confusion." WR - "I have learned that financial confusion is normal." TH - "Cash, money, wealth, riches. It is all screwed up!"

Wow. That's enough to get anyone stirred up. Or maybe depressed if that was where we stopped. Don't stop here!

Take some deep breaths. That tapping was for bringing up a lot of the junk so that it can begin to be moved out, alright? Now we're going to shift into some tapping for opening new space.

EB - "I'm aware now, I have a lot of things that don't work for me about money." SE - "Maybe, maybe, if I have an awareness of what isn't working that can help me notice what could work for me." UE - "I'm willing to notice, I'm more than willing to notice what has not worked for me was not working for me. UN - "I'm willing to notice what isn't working for other people too; especially when they're telling me it does work." On the CH - "I'm willing to know what I know about money. I'm willing to know that I know many things."

CB - "I open my mind to knowing this for me." UA - "There are actions to take AND actions to NOT take with MY money." LP - "Maybe my past with money was not my own relationship with money. I can see where I've been running everyone else's relationship patterns with money." WR - "I am ready to be present with money in a new way and open to my intuition here." TH - "I've been mimicking everyone else's patterns with money and that isn't working.

Deep Slow Breath.

Tapping at the EB - "I choose now to choose for me. I get to choose, and I choose for me." SE - "I'm willing for things to change. I am ready for my money to contribute to my life." UE - "I'm willing to have money and ease." UN - "I could have money. I could even have things go well for me!?" CH - "Other people might be upset with me."

CB - "I am willing to have money." UA - "I'm willing to have my own relationship and find out what works for me with my finances." LP - "This is new, but it could be fun to have new outcomes with my money." WR - "I am ready to get to know money in new ways and have my relationship grow." TH - "My relationship with money is mine to choose and create."

Breathe. Check your SUDS level. If it has gone up, keep tapping. If your SUDS level is going down, you could make a note to recheck later and let the topic rest right now to allow for integration.

Remember, if your SUDS level seems to stagnate on a topic, reference the section about the Gamut Point Technique and make sure you are having enough water.

Receiving

Looking back to the process for harmonizing with a substance. Have you been holding onto a coin? Here are some follow up questions.

What amount of money makes you uncomfortable? Have you noticed, if someone handed you a $20 bill, is that reasonable? Did you need to earn it? Did you have to compensate them somehow? Would you be like "Oh, thank you!" and put it in your pocket. Or are you more likely to ask, "Do you need change?" Are you mostly good with $20? Okay, how about $50, $100, $500 or $1000?

At what point are you buying into something or maybe selling something? You will want to know what the deal or agreement is. It brings up everything about contracts and agendas. Or, you know, is this *actually* a gift? Is this a big enough amount that I'll have to report to the IRS? Is this something that I'm gonna owe you and have to pay it back later?

Where is that threshold? Where do you start to hold your breath? Is it $100, $1000? Make a note. What are the sensations in your body?

Now, is there a difference with the money being electronic or physical? What is the feeling for you if money is coming directly into your account? Is that just "Oh, cool. Yay!" Versus if the money came in physically handed to you as a stack of cash. Is it about the same? Does that idea of holding physical money make you feel anxious?

Do you anticipate theft because you have it 'for real' and you're walking around with it?

Is there an upper limit on what feels normal in your accounts? Electronically, is there a certain number at the top for your savings, like about $900, where you anticipate bad news? Such as "Well, here's an unexpected bill to knock me back down to zero" or into the negative?

Is there a lower limit, a number in debt that you're comfortable with, and that you return to regularly?

The number(s) past which you're suddenly uncomfortable having in your account are your set points. The lower set point can be around zero, but it doesn't have to be at zero.

For example, a parent that runs life at an ongoing deficit of minus $10,000 will resonate with "I've been in debt forever. This is my life." Even if they never specifically speak with their children, their habits and mindset will likely transfer to the children as a starting point for their future money reality.

Likewise, a parent who regularly has a financial surplus and feels congruent with keeping all debts paid in a timely manner will imprint their children with that money mindset and the matching financial habits that will give them a template for having similarly positive monetary outcomes.

For either perspective, when the account gets very much over or under the comfortable financial parameters, they will have an internal need to adjust things. "Oh, I gotta do something to change this!" Having to 'hustle' on occasion, while not bad, is still not a healthy dynamic and flowing relationship with money.

The good news here is that your financial set points can be moved higher! You may have begun by mirroring the financial patterns that you inherited, but you don't have to stay there. You also don't have to wait for things to get worse before you are free to create and generate your future.

Looking at this pattern of financial set points, note your SUDS level and start tapping through the acupoints. Remember to breathe and adjust the words to suit your needs.

You will benefit from this tapping even if you are using generic numbers.

EB - "I'm okay with $10,000 in debt [insert whatever your number is]. I'm okay with this much (not) in my account." SE - "This is normal for me" UE - "I can be comfortable here. I am someone who has that much debt/money." UN - "That's fine with me." CH - "If I go too much over that, or under that number, suddenly I'm not okay with it!"

CB - "There's something going on here. I have a preset number locked in there somewhere. I marked and labeled [this number] as acceptable and [that number] as too much." UA - "I don't like being limited this way. Even though it seems safe to stay within these parameters." LP - "It bothers me that I've been creating and recreating these patterns that I didn't even choose on purpose for my money!" WR - "I like feeling safe. I don't like feeling stuck." TH - "I can see the value of having a preset resting point and auto piloted habits to run my life. There are positive and negative limitations with using set points."

Tapping at the EB - "I have these parameters; these places that have just been running everything." SE - I have places where money is acceptable..." UE - "and beyond that it's not acceptable." UN - "These financial parameters." CH - "Who decided this?"

CB - "At some point, consciously or unconsciously, I agreed to maintain these set points as my reality." UA - "What if I could change my set points?" LP - "What if this holding pattern could change?" WR - "I would like to upgrade my life. I am ready for my financial reality to improve." TH - "Could I have more fun if I moved my set points?"

EB - "What if I could enjoy my money? Could I learn to have fun with money?" SE - "What if money is willing to have healthy fun with me?" UE - "What would that look like? How would I feel if my parameters moved higher?" UN - "Feeling stuck is no fun. These parameters, these set points were just given to me." CH - "I received them blindly, and probably before the age of two! This isn't even about me."

CB - "I've duplicated them. What would I like to have?" UA - "Who else could I duplicate?" LP - "What else can I choose to duplicate and install for myself now?" WR - "I'm not obligated to follow old patterns, what would I like to choose?" TH - "Maybe I could bring the vision of my successful self to mind. What would that be like, to be more free in and as myself with money now?"

Breathe. check in on your SUDS levels.

How do you feel thinking about a large sum of money just sitting in front of you? How do you feel about receiving a large increase? What about a large bill? What words or phrases need more attention with a few more rounds of tapping?

We've been daisy-chaining. When you just branch off on the next thing, the next and the next thing… It can be confusing, but sifting through all the connected vocabulary is usually where I have found the chord of the major issue that can be addressed with EFT.

If you go to say something out loud, but then you cough or you choke and suddenly can't say it; that's probably your topic! You'll want to spend a bit more time pulling up those thoughts and tapping through any related memories or sensations in your body.

Ask, "When did I agree to this? Who am I being when I choose this way of behaving with money? How old am I feeling when I sit with this topic?" Those are great questions to spark your mind for rounds of independent tapping.

When we were kids, many things seemed to be free to us. Was that freedom emotionally clean and clear or was there a hidden agenda, like a bribe that we had to repay later? Was there a gradual or an abrupt change as you became 18 years old? At what point were you introduced to the need to work and earn an hourly wage?

Do you carry a sense of indebtedness, worthlessness or the idea that you are a burden to someone?

Before we can talk, there is exposure to the idea of giving and receiving or buying and selling. Was there a tally being kept of all the things that you owe to the family, to the neighbors, to the church, school, or community?

41

Now there's something that you used to be able to do. Most places will no longer have a small credit line in the corner store. We used to go in on a family name tally and you'd leave with what you needed. You go in, they write it down, then someone will make the payment and settle the tab later. There was trust and co-operation to build communities.

Things around us keep changing. The rules are not the same and many of us walk around carrying anxiety and heaviness in us as we worry about debt and keeping up with everything on our own.

Adapting to Change

This is a new topic. Let's begin with the set-up phrase, tapping on the side of the hand. KC - "I don't like feeling like this. All these places where I've been misled, all of these places where I've been trained into habits that don't serve me, I see those now." Breathe deeply, in and out. "I see those patterns and I love and accept myself. I choose to accept all of me. I know that this pattern has been part of my life. There's all this stuff where I was misinformed and trained with poor habits. And I accept myself now."

EB - "I've been misled." SE - "Misinformed and uneducated." UE - "Financial abuse has been part of my life." UN - "I have been misinformed and misdirected." CH - "I have been manipulated." CB - "Hidden agendas with money have been normal." UA - "All of this twisting." LP - "All of this bastardization around money and finances." WR - "There is insanity around money, and we think that that is normal!" TH - "There is so much that does not work for me about the way I have been relating to money."

Take a deep breath. Rest here for a few minutes.

As you find that you have other specific words arising, I recommend that you continue to tap as you tell your story out loud. You'll find that there are other pieces of it, other details that need to be witnessed and released. Such as, "I really don't like owing people! All this owing people!" and then tap through all the points with a reminder phrase like, "I grew up owing money to people. It was just this constant, ever present, 'We owe people.' We have debt. There's no way to get out of it or ahead of it." So yes, if that energy is coming up, go ahead and tap as you let yourself feel into what is there. Keep going. Keep talking and tapping.

If you're tapping, you're telling your body to clear and reset the meridian pathways that feed your internal organs. By tapping you're resetting your whole body to have clarity and peace at the same time as being present with the topics of money. Soon you will be able to talk about these things; think about your choices and NOT trip into a reaction.

As you continue tapping you will find that you do not go into mental significance and physical contraction as frequently and that if you do your system will remember tapping and recover more quickly. You can be calm and clear headed around subjects that used to spin you out. You can make an informed choice versus just repeating the dysfunctional patterns over and over again.

Tapping at the side of the hand, KC - "I have been embarrassed about money and I accept who I am. I see where I was raised to be ashamed of money and I love and accept who I am now. I deeply and completely love and accept myself even though I was raised to hide things about money, keep secrets and feel embarrassed."

You are welcome to tap on both sides at the same time, but it is not necessary.

Tapping through the points, EB - "All of the secrecy about money; the secrecy keeping me stuck in shame." SE - "Secrets and shame about money." UE - "There is secrecy and silence about money." UN - "Secrecy. Silence and hidden, shameful things about money." CH - "There are shameful things being done with money." CB - "Sometimes money is dirty. People who have lots of money

44

can be dirty and rotten!" UA - "I know it's true! There are shameful things that happen with money!" LP - "There are painful, shameful, secret things that happen around large sums of money." WR - "It is disgusting! I don't want to think about how horrible people can be with money." TH - "All of this; avoiding money to avoid shame, avoiding money to avoid evil and darkness."

Deep breath. Close your eyes tight. Open them and look around the room. Wiggle your fingers. Shake out your arms. Roll your shoulders.

Take another deep breath and then as you breathe out choose to relax all the way down to your toes.

So now, look back to our topic about being lied to, misdirected and uneducated, even embarrassed and ashamed around the topic of money - is there that same feeling on it? Are there specific events that come to mind? How old were you? How old did you feel? Who was involved? What did they tell you in that moment that has stayed with you? Did that remind you of an earlier experience or of another person? Breathe. Write it down.

Each one of your life events that has emotional intensity is worth taking 5 - 10 minutes to witness, assess the SUDS level and tap through the points. As you verbalize what you remember, what you felt then and what you think and feel about it now, the snarled electromagnetic components of those thoughts and feelings can be dissipated and released from your physiology.

As you put down the weight of your financial past you will be lighter and brighter in your ability to think clearly and easily adjust to changes around you.

Being able to respond with calm clarity and self-assurance in any stressful situation is an enviable skill that you can access and develop through the application of Emotional Freedom Techniques.

Navigating Discomfort

Beginning on the sore spot or on the side of the hand. Repeat after me, KC - "It seems like everyone around me has all these same problems with money and right now I choose to accept who I am. I deeply and completely love and accept myself and I don't want to be financially stuck like the people around me! Money is a big uncomfortable topic and I love who I am."

EB - Money is uncomfortable. Talking about money is uncomfortable." SE - "I can tell that the people around me are still uncomfortable with money." UE - "Thinking about changing my money patterns and habits is uncomfortable." UN - "Changing my behavior is probably... definitely gonna make the people around me uncomfortable!" CH - "If I change myself, who knows what happens next?!"

CB - "They might feel hurt or angry! They might want me to stop changing so they can be who they are used to being with money." UA - "I've been validating other people's realities by matching them in their money realities." LP - "I see what I've been doing. This is not kind to me." WR - "I've been going along with what I was told-whether or not it works for me." TH - "Talking about being stuck is uncomfortable. Thinking about making things change is very uncomfortable!"

EB - "I choose to breathe deeply and slowly. I will take the time to spend and invest it in making sure that I am taken care of right now." SE - "I can come back to following my breath and tapping through the points whenever anything gets stressful for me." UE - "I can slow down and be present with my body. It is good to breathe and tap." UN - "Even if I am not sure what to do next. Even when I am confused or overwhelmed, I can take a long slow breath and do some gentle tapping." CH - "I have the option to soothe my own nervous system and reset my breathing patterns."

CB - "I've been in the habit of being stressed out when the people around me are stressed, fearful or angry." UA - "I know that I do not have to mirror their emotions and match their behaviors in my own body." LP - "I can witness the people around me and follow my breath to find my center and tap into my calm resourceful mind." WR - "I have been in the habit of holding my breath, matching the people around me, and waiting for what they will choose." TH – "That has not always gone well for me. I have choices to make here about my financial future."

EB - "I can be aware of what other people feel and choose to respect my thoughts and feelings too. I can choose now to change my financial reality." SE - "That might take noticing. What is true for me? What has been true for me about money?" UE - "It'll probably take asking questions and noticing how I feel." UN - "This is new for me to notice my little background thoughts. I am willing to try tapping through the tangle of thoughts and feelings that arise." CH - "I will get to form new habits and learn new things about myself and about money."

CB - "The people around me might or might not want to change. I know I can change even if they don't change." UA - "Change can be uncomfortable, and I know that something else is possible for me." LP - "I have been uncomfortable before and this change will be something that I am creating in myself, for myself." WR - "Change happens every day, whether or not I participate. There are changes that I can make on purpose to improve my life. I choose to focus on that." TH - "All of this stuff about money. Everything about changing money can come to me and through my life with grace now."

EB - "Discomfort has stopped me in the past." SE - "I don't like to feel uncomfortable, and I don't like to feel wrong." UE - "I want my life to improve but I don't want to upset anyone." UN - "I can make small changes and gain a lot of information." CH - "I am allowed to tap as often as necessary to move through all of this at my own pace."

CB - "I could even get a tapping buddy, coach or friend to talk me through big emotions or hesitations and doubts with this content." UA - These topics of financial abuse and financial freedom are big topics!" LP - "I've had years of convolution with all of this. It is more than OK to not unwind everything all at once!" WR - "I am free to tap for whatever arises around money and move through this content at my own pace." TH - "I get to decide how quickly or slowly I change my thoughts and feelings about money."

Take a deep breath. Maybe get some water. Look around the room and let that content move.

As a reference point, I want you to really check in about what 'normal' looks like. What amount of money, as poverty or luxury makes you uncomfortable? And is there a difference with the electronic amount -like looking at the number on a screen versus holding physical money. At what point do you freak out and not feel safe to walk around if you have 'that much' cash on you?

Another side of this too, at what point in expenditures and debt do you get uncomfortable? I found out recently that I have been perfectly happy with lots of debt. Honestly, I didn't know that about myself.

Carrying debt is not okay with many, many people. I assumed I was uncomfortable with debt. It was in playing a silly game, wearing name tags at an event, that I realized my whole body relaxed when I got to introduce myself as the "Negative Billionaire!" It brought me to the realization that I grew up with my parents deeply in debt and avoiding phone calls from debt collectors. That was imprinted on me as 'normal life' and pinned my financial setpoint way down in the red.

Debt wasn't something that anyone talked about or chose to share the details with the kids. I really didn't consciously understand how poor we were in my childhood until much later in my life.

That is what we are looking for right now. What unnamed and unspoken truths did you learn and file away for how to be with your money as an adult?

Make a note. Is there a SUDS level associated with that number? Is it something that brings embarrassment or pride in you? Take a breath. Let's tap.

KC - "All the places I have been misled, misinformed, and manipulated, abused, and neglected. Blamed, shamed, and guilted around money … Oh, holy crap! There's so much inherited financial stupidity, and I am choosing to love me. Right here, right now, I am awesome. I'm choosing to do something about this. It's a big mess. There's a lot of discomfort with all this money stuff and I love who I am anyway."

EB - "Financial discomfort." SE - "I am uncomfortable with money discussions." UE - "There it is, I have witnessed abuse and neglect with money." UN - "Hardship with money." CH - "I've neglected money. I've ignored money."

CB - " I've blamed money. I've avoided dealing with money. I've been blamed for the money problems other people have! Sometimes I blame other people for my money issues too." UA - "There's so much shame. There's so much here that we're not supposed to talk about." LP - "Is it any wonder that this is uncomfortable." WR - "My whole family has their own weirdness about money." TH - "Money guilt. Money Shame. No wonder I've been confused."

EB - "I've been misled." SE - "I've been lied to." UN - "Money is stupid. Is it really?" UN - "Or maybe it is the people that are stupid with money. People are stupid with money." CH - "Sometimes I'm stupid with my money too. Money is just money."

CB - "I obviously have to make myself stupid. I have to participate in this reality." UA - "What amount of money makes me uncomfortable? What about an amount that would be comfortable? Was it $10,000? $10,000 received or $10,000 owed?" LP - "How much money do I need to have in my account for me to feel comfortable?" WR - "Is there an amount of money, set aside, that would tell my physiology and mind to relax and feel safe?" TH - "But hush! We can't talk about money. No one expects to actually be comfortable with money, do they?"

EB - "We all know that money is shameful, and wanting it is wrong." SE - "Receiving money is shameful somehow. It's humiliating to need money." UE - "But giving money, that's the thing to do." UN - "Can I breathe easily if I don't have money? or is it only a sigh or a groan that I am allowed?" CH - "All the stupidity with money. All this stupidity about money."

CB - "It's so stupid. I'm so tired of all the stupidity." UA - "All the lies and all the misinformation, abuse and neglect, blame, shame and guilt around money." LP - "This is crazy that we live this way." WR - "I have not wanted to see all the financial insanity." TH - "I see it now. It can be changed now, in me and for me. I am willing for this to change."

EB - "This distortion is not mine, not really." SE - "I've been carrying it around, but I know it's not who I am." UE - "I am willing to know who I am." UN - "Maybe the energy of money would like to work with me." CH - "I'm not like all the other people."

CB - "I'm willing to have money flow to me and through my life with ease." UA - "I wonder how having money will be different as I am choosing to show up for myself now?" LP - "I am opening space for flowing with vitality in my finances." WR - "I choose to flow with new ideas and sustainable actions." TH - "I am ready to flow with financial grace. I look forward to experiencing that."

Deep breath. Wiggle. Stretch. Do you need sunlight, movement, water, sugar, or salt?

These practices burn through water, sugar, and salt in our bodies as we alter the signals along our electrical pathways, to clear out the stagnation, and choose emotional freedom.

Check in with yourself. Be sure to support your body in this reality alteration process.

If you are feeling tired after tapping, a short nap could be advisable while your body propagates all the mental and emotional updates and attempts integration in new ways.

Connecting with Resource States

This segment is about using a tool called 'Ask & Receive' that was developed by Sandi Radomski.

For more about Sandi and her work with healing bodies, visit AllergyAntidotes.com

Her technique, referenced here, is beautifully amplified with tapping. We are going to use her scripted prompts for the talking, so tap wherever you like.

You can move through the points in the standard sequence or move out of order and bounce around. If you feel like it's time to move on to the next place, go ahead and move on to the next place. Or you could choose to tap a specific place like your collarbone or sternum the whole time. Remember to be gentle as you tap.

First, identify what the problem is and put it into a sentence. For us right now, something like "I am very stressed about money." "I am anxious about money." "I am having trouble paying my bills." or "My body is holding on to fear." "I do not know how to manage money" and "I do not know how to deal with people and things around money." would work. Each of these should be processed separately. You are giving your mind and body a focused statement - simple pictures & ideas work best.

Follow one topic, one premise and focus statement all the way through. Note your SUDS level on the chosen topic.

Continue to the tapping sequence and say aloud something like, "Even though I am currently very stressed about____, I KNOW that there is a part of My Being that knows how to relax, let go & resolve this challenge. In fact,

54

I know there is a part of me that has the resources necessary to resolve [this] and has already done so."

Next, while tapping, say out loud some version of "I ask for that part of me, that has this knowledge & has already resolved this situation, to inform my body, mind, and soul of this change; how to heal & that this trauma has stopped happening. Inform me that I am safe, and that it is safe for me to be in my body now."

You could add "Please inform my body, mind, and soul on all levels and in all directions of time that these things have changed for the better."

Keep tapping through the point and acknowledge the progress by saying "I know that this part of me is willing to do so and has already begun to share this energy and information with me now."

Then, still tapping, "I choose to receive this energy and information transfer in my body, mind and soul."

Close with, "Energy transfer is now complete." You can also give thanks to all aspects of you that shared or contributed in any way to this process of healing.

After that, it is time to check in again with your original statement and SUDS level.

See what comes up next (as related issues) to take through this Ask & Receive process or continue tapping for those with the standard set up phrase and tapping sequence.

Notice what you feel about this idea of calling for assistance. Listen for any quiet thoughts or feelings that are running contrary energies in the background noise of your mind. Consider making a calendar entry to revisit your tapping topic with the Ask & Receive process.

Addressing feelings of grief, anger, abandonment, and general distrust of Divinity can be very pivotal for clearing out blocks to receiving long term, sustainable prosperity.

Clearing Stupidity and Lies

There are many questions and tools woven into this material that I learned from over a decade of taking classes with Access Consciousness™ For more about their books and training visit AccessConsciousness.com and TheClearingStatement.com

For this next tapping segment, we will use a term that may bother you, it is "stupidity." As a state of being unwise, it can be used to denote unconsciousness, anti-consciousness and lack of awareness maintained as though it is more real and true than who we truly are in our infinite capacities.

This question, like most from Access, is not meant to be specifically answered. We are using it as a way to bring up energy and gain awareness. It is worded in an odd way to help trip irrational things. "What stupidity am I using to keep this [problem] financial mess in place as reality -Am I choosing?"

Notice. Did something come up around the word stupidity? Do you believe that you have been stupid with your money? What events come to mind right now? What are the sensations in your body? Make note of those events and your current SUDS level, 0-10.

Rub circles at the sore spot or tap along at the side of the hand.

KC - "Even though there's a financial mess right now, I know I can choose, and I do choose to love and accept myself. Even though the whole topic of money has been a mess, I choose to love and accept myself. I choose now to relax and breathe…relax and breathe even though my financial reality has been a mess."

EB - "Such a mess." SE - "All this financial mess." UE - "There's more of a mess here than anything I made." UN - "I walked in on somebody else's mess." CH - Deep breath. "This mess. This stupidity! It's not all mine."

CB - "I'm aware of a big problem about money. It feels so big." UA - "There's a mess here." LP - "There's a financial mess here." WR - "Money has been a stupidly messy subject for a long time." TH - Financial stupidity. Financial mess."

EB - "Stupidity. Chaos even!" SE - "Messy stupidity with money. This is so stupid." UE - "Financial stupidity." Deep breath. UN - "Such a mess with money." CH - "It all feels sooo much bigger than me. This stupidity is so much more than I can process."

CB - "Bigger than anything I could ever resolve." UA - "Huge mess." LP - "I couldn't sort it out even if I wanted to!" WR - "The insanity is epic. The stupidity is ridiculously dense." TH - "All of this financial crap."

EB - "If I didn't make this mess maybe I don't have to clean it up? Maybe…." SE - "There's so much content here." UE - "Other people have been willing and allowed to just walk away and leave the financial mess." UN - Deep breath. "What if it's not mine to solve?" CH - "I have all this awareness about stupidity with money."

CB - "Maybe I could know the difference now? Maybe I do know the difference between theirs and mine? What is my responsibility? And what is clearly not mine." UA - "What is within the realm of possibility for me to choose?" LP - "Maybe I've been learning from the stupidity around me." WR - "What if, I can witness stupidity and not need to duplicate it into my own life?" TH - "What am I aware of here? What is simply there for me to walk away from?"

EB - "All this stupidity with money. I am willing to release all this crap." SE - "I can know that it's there and choose for my life. I can be aware of everyone's financial mess and choose to generate my life." UN - "I am willing to release the patterns of financial abuse and all the residue of it in my life." CH - "I am willing to open a new space."

CB - "I'm willing to be open for new ideas to flow to me and through me." UA - "I could even have a new education!" LP - "I can choose to connect with people that actually know what they're doing with money." WR - "I have so much capacity to learn new habits when I release what isn't working." TH - "I choose to be open to new outcomes with money and wisdom combined."

EB - "I am willing to release financial abuse in all its forms and applications." SE - "I'm willing to release all this crap that does not serve my financial growth." Take a deep breath. UE - "I can choose what works for me." UN - "How I think and feel about money is my choice." CH - "I have choices to make as I move forward."

CB - "I can generate my life." UA - "I am part of a choosing generation." LP - "We are aware and choosing now. I am releasing the burden of financial abuse." WR - "I let go of old ways and set myself free." TH - "I have the option to make new choices and follow new pathways for my financial health now."

Pause. Take a deep breath. Wiggle wiggle wiggle.

That was an interesting progression. We had a starting point to acknowledge some of the stupidity that has been going on within and around us and then we just followed that through to see where the thread of tapping and daisy-chaining would land. That is a wonderful way to explore your thoughts and feelings.

Start tapping and talking and keep going; tapping on whatever comes up and whatever comes to mind. At some point, you shift over from acknowledging and witnessing the junk, over into opening the space for possibility and hope that things can change. Stick with tapping through the points as your words start to feel lighter. Then you can move into programming, tapping in the affirmations and possibilities for yourself.

That's one of the things you're going to want to pay attention to as it is happening. On the one hand, it's easy to tap superficially and not bring up the junk because it is uncomfortable! Who wants to do that? But avoiding discomfort robs you of actually moving the energy around the really deep, heavy emotional content. Passing through that challenge will bring you to have the experience of emotional freedom in a bigger way.

Then when you find relief don't stop the rounds of tapping too soon! Once you clear out a bunch of the heavy gunky stuff, if you stop right there, you're just in a neutral space and you could shift into Drive.

You can use tapping to take your reality out of reverse, into neutral and all the way into a commitment for stepping forward into new pathways. By using EFT, you are helping your body to become congruent with the possibilities for a generative future.

60

We are going to continue the tapping for twisted stupidities and bastardization; all the inventions and lies about money.

Tapping on the side of the hand. KC - "Twisted stupidities? This reality is so full of lies, this reality is so polarized, and I know that that's not who I am. I deeply and completely love and accept myself. Even though there are lots of lies in this reality. Even though there are lots of lies today, there are twisted stupidities about money and financial abuse, in particular. Right now, I choose to hold myself as safe within myself."

EB - "Twisted stupidities running around money." SE - "Bastardization of money." UE - "Inventions and lies about finances and who can access wealth." UN - "Receiving has sometimes been convoluted and painful." CH - "All these twisted stupidities."

CB - "I'm aware of the bastardization of money." UA - "I've experienced painful things because of the lies in this reality." LP - "Twisted stupidities have caused me confusion and pain." WR - "There is so much twisted up and confused about money in this reality." TH - "I can't keep all of this stupidity inside of me."

EB - "I was never meant to internalize all this chaos and insanity." SE - "Twisted stupidities don't make sense!" UE - "Taking them inside my body to better understand them does not work. They are still twisted and all stupid." UN - "All that that is. Everywhere I've internalized lies about money, I release it now." CH - "All that I've done to align and agree with this reality and make it mine; I release it now."

CB - "I claim full permission to let all of it go."
UA - "There is so much grief and so many lies all wrapped
up and twisted together about money." LP - "All the grief
and all the lies of money can leave my body now." WR - "I
choose to relax and allow these convoluted things to
dissipate from my mind and my body." TH - "I will no
longer be bound by the twisted stupidities and lies around
money."

EB - "There is the energy of lack and struggle." SE
- "There isn't enough to go around? Maybe that's one of the
lies of money too." UE - "Maybe lack is true and maybe it
isn't." UN - "Is lack of anything a reality? Deep breath. CH
- "Scarcity. Lack. Twisted stupidities. Lies and confusion
around money."

CB - "Is it true? I've been told that there isn't
enough." UA - "Do I believe that line of thought? 'I'll
never be done. I'll never make the ends meet.'" LP -
"There's always the foreboding of 'another shoe waiting to
drop.' There are so many consequences for every choice
and action." WR - "Sheesh! No wonder people choose to
numb themselves with addictions and distractions." TH -
"The stupidity and lies around money are endlessly
twisted."

EB - "This is so heavy and draining." SE - "I can
feel stupid just talking about how stupid it all is. Stupid
financial abuses that pass for normal." UE - "Financial
abuse from other people and from myself!" UN - "I've
hired people, consciously or not, to help me maintain this
hardship as my reality." CH - "I love this reality and all the
complexity! I am so entertained by the manufactured
scarcity around me."

CB - "I hate this reality. I love to hate it sooo much!" UA - "I love it. I love it!" LP - "I love to hate this reality." WR - "I hate to love all the lies about money." TH - "I need it. I need it! I don't need it."

EB - "Who would I be without these twisted stupidities?" SE - "I'm so twisted up with all the lies of money." UE - "That's it! I'm a financial pretzel." UN - "I can't possibly unlearn all of it!" CH - "I'll never know enough to be doing a good job." Deep breath.

CB - "There's no point in starting to unlearn and relearn everything. I'll do it wrong anyway." UA - "I'll do it wrong." LP - "Such a financial pickle I am in!" WR - "I don't know what to learn. No one can teach me." TH - "How am I supposed to change? I can't just magically drop the old and know new things! Can I?"

EB - " My 'knower' is wrong." SE - "My 'knower' is right." UE - "My companions are wrong." UN - "My companions are right." CH - "My dad is right."

CB - "My dad is wrong." UA - "My mom is right, and my mom is wrong." LP - "I have been right, and I have been wrong." WR - "Both and neither and somewhere in between." TH - "I am right. I am wrong. I've always been right. I've always been wrong. I've never been right, and I've never been wrong."

EB - "What if I could function in new ways?" SE - "I would like to have new and pleasant experiences with money." UE - "I am willing to change my money patterns gradually and completely." UN - "The people around me may or may not change with me." CH - "My money reality is already shifting."

CB - "My past is my past. I can let old things fall away." UA - "My future is ready for me to shape and to embrace." LP - "I have space and time to make adjustments as I learn what works for me." WR - "Relationships grow over time. I can invest in building a healthy relationship with money." TH - "I choose to take inspired actions with my money that grow my resources and build my income."

Take a deep breath. Long slow inhalation. Long slow exhalation.

Check in. Does any of that need more attention? Do you have a specific thread of memory or emotional intensity that could be pulled up and further unraveled right now with a little more tapping?

Keeping Secrets or Finding Divine Timing

How many secrets are we keeping from each other and from ourselves? Do you trust yourself? How much does a habit of keeping secrets and hiding things lead you to not trust others? Have we learned to be suspicious for good reasons or simply from paranoia? Because if you know you are keeping secrets then it is easy to think, and see and feel, through that clouded lens and say, "They're probably keeping secrets too!" Let's tap for all of that.

Side of the hand. Repeat after me, "Even though the world is full of secrecy and there are so many hidden things about finances, I choose to lovingly accept myself. I embrace all of myself, even though I don't want to. Nope, I don't want to! There are too many secrets. I don't know what's true anymore, and I accept who I am. I know I have good reasons for my confusion and my suspicions. I know there have been a lot of people contributing to my financial mess. And I love who I am right now."

EB - "Financial secrets." SE - "Hidden money." UE - "Stolen money and broken promises." UN - "Secrets kept. 'On pain of death!' I must keep this secret." CH - "Or is it, 'On pain of death!' I must tell the secret?" Deep breath.

CB - "Mixed committal obligations with all these secrets." UA - "These secrets about money." LP - "My secrets. Their secrets." WR - "Her secrets. His secrets." TH - "Where money comes from. Where money goes. I'm not allowed to know. I am not allowed to say."

EB - "Money is hidden and mysterious." SE - "Money doesn't just grow on trees!" UE - "All this money secrecy." UN - "I feel so alone." CH - "Keeping all of these secrets keeps me isolated."

65

CB - "Money isn't something we talk about freely. Maybe we talk about spending or needing to save or needing to make more of it." UA - "Keeping money. Having money isn't something we talk about openly." LP - "It hasn't been safe to have money." WR - "It isn't a good idea to ask too many questions about money." TH - " I know that there are hidden resources and hidden treasures on the planet."

EB - "Hidden debt is more common." SE - "We've all experienced the horror of finding a hidden cost. The surprise extra fee." UE - "I expect hidden expenses now." UN - "All this, and 'Surprise! You've incurred another debt!' is getting really old." CH - "Shock and trauma with money."

CB - "Shock and trauma because of financial secrets." UA - "Shock and trauma about financial decisions." LP - "Keeping secrets. Telling secrets." WR - "Selling secrets. TH - "Exposing 'top secret' secrets."

EB - "Financial secrecy. Does it serve a purpose?" SE - "Financial isolation." UE - "Financial obligations." UN - "All these secrets twisting me up inside." CH - "Secrecy for the sake of secrecy."

CB - "Secrecy to keep secrecy alive." Deep breath. UA - "This is exhausting." LP - "Can we be done with all the twisted stupidities, lies and secrecy around money yet?" WR - "This is so heavy and so dense." TH - "I'm ready for this to change in my world. I'm willing for change to be graceful too."

So now let's give it permission to come up and actually be uninstalled. We are going to combine tapping with a clearing from Access Consciousness™

EB - "All the known and unknown content about what keeps money as a secret from me." SE - "All the bindings, contracts and commitments." UE - "All the curses, bondings, oaths." UN - "Or blood oaths, known and unknown, that are right now in place around me." CH - "All of that, that is right now screwing up my life with money."

CB - "I choose to revoke, recant, rescind." UA - "I now renounce, denounce, destroy and uncreate whatever that is." LP - "In me, on me or around me; across all time, space dimensions and realities." WR - "I reclaim my choices." TH - "I reclaim my sovereign nature and my access to the Divine Source for my creation."

KC - "I love and accept all of me. I dare myself to love me even with all of this unnamed financial bogus that has been happening all around me. Even with all of this financial stress and confusion, even though everything feels shrouded and mysterious, or outright fucked up, I know that I am loved and I love me!"

EB - "Unnamed financial abuse." SE - "Abuse. Preverbal, non-verbal, and verbal financial abuse." UE - "preverbal and non-verbal financial abuse." UN - " I don't even have words for all of what I've been through." CH - "So much twisted stupidity wrapped up in maintaining financial abuse."

CB - "Financial abuse. Financial abuse has been embedded in my body." UA - "Unnamed, unknown, unspoken." LP - "Everything unseen and unheard." WR - "The residue of financial abuse in me that was unacknowledged and unwitnessed has permission to leave me now." TH - "Wait! No!? Who am I without that? I'm gonna keep it forever!?"

EB - "Oh hell no! I am not keeping this insanity in my body any longer!" SE - "I have to keep it forever. I promised to keep it close and quiet for my family!" UE - "I don't know who I am without it! I have to keep the pain to be who I am." UN - "So many promises, so many timelines all mixed up." CH - "Heaps of crap. Layer after layer after layer after layer after layer."

CB - "It's so thick. It's so deep. I can hardly breathe." UA - "The residue of unnamed financial abuse. I want to scream!" LP - "This is stupid. This is insane." WR - "No wonder we are so dysfunctional around money." TH - "There is so much financial abuse in the world. I don't even know where to start."

EB - "Wow. It is astonishing how dysfunctional things have become." SE - "I don't even have words for all of this financial nonsense." UE - "But it's distorting my life in upsetting ways." UN - "Distortion has been ruining my life." CH - "Well, crap."

CB - "Twisted stupidities seem to be unavoidable." UA - "Bottomless lies about lies." Deep breath. LP - "The lies of money are pervasive and endless. WR - "I know that they are there AND they are not mine to solve." TH - "I call myself back from the abyss of that twisted stupidity with money and the lies of money."

Shifting gears a little now. We are going to tap for choosing our timing and having allowance. Are you willing to go there? Creating your own timing versus waiting for others. Being aware of others and not hung up on their interesting points of view.

Can you be aware of their hesitations, yet hold on to choosing what works for you? Which means maybe letting go of all your own interesting points of view. This is not solving the past, not projecting, and expecting the future. Being present and adaptable in an ongoing way.

KC - "Timing and allowance? Both together isn't something I've really experienced and right now, for 10 seconds, I choose to love and accept myself. I choose to love my own timing and have full allowance even though it seems beyond me." Deep breath. "I love who I am! In fact, I will choose to love me more than I ever have for these next few minutes. Even though this is new, I choose to know that timing and allowance are things I can choose to embrace."

EB - "Time for timing. But what is it to 'have allowance' for myself? SE - "Fuck allowance. I don't need to 'have allowance'." UE - "They need to 'have allowance' for me!" UN - "Who wants to have good timing?" CH - "Who decides what good timing is anyway?"

CB - "What is good timing?" UA - "I think good timing is moving in my own time. I should get to choose for myself." LP - "Good timing or bad timing." WR - "There is a lot of judgment and perspective about what is good or bad timing. That's interesting." TH - "Timing is in relation to me. Timing is about working with my body and navigating my physical reality."

EB - "Maybe I did 'miss the boat.' They said I missed out." UE - "Maybe I'll never catch up to where I think I ought to be." UN - "Who says I need to catch up?" CH - "Maybe I didn't want to get on that boat anyway."

CB - "Financial timing. What is that?" UA - "Financial timing." LP - "Timing with finances and money." WR - "Finding my pace and my timing with my money." TH - "What if my body knows what to do and when to take action?"

EB - "Financial timing. Divine timing. Are they the same? Are they different?" SE - "What about Divine financial timing?" UE - "My financial advisor could be the Universe? Good Financial timing... Am I waiting for Divine timing?" UN - "One day. One day Divinity will grant me my abundance!" CH - "No it won't. Grace is for other people."

CB - "Yes it will! I've worked so hard!" UA - "The Universe loves me." LP - "The Universe hates me!" WR - "The Universe loves who I am." TH - "Maybe it isn't about the Universe hating or loving anything or anyone."

EB - "Do I hate me?" SE - "Do I love me? Could I love myself? Is that allowed?" UE - "Can I have patience, acceptance and allowance for myself?" UN - "No. I can't. No. I won't." CH - " I've never had patience, acceptance and allowance for myself."

CB - "I've never seen anyone else with allowance." UA - "Maybe I have, maybe I do know someone to reference." LP - "I know that there are kind and loving people in the world. Do they also have money?" WR - "I can choose to show myself kindness and compassion." TH - "What if all of my 'feeling like a mess' is because I have an awareness of the mess in the world around me? What if I do know what would work for me?"

EB - "What if I do know lots of things?" SE - "What if I am aware of timing?" UE - "What if I am aware of what it is to choose acceptance and allowance? What if I am aware of possibilities?" UN - "I could choose something new." CH - "I could allow myself to be guided in new ways."

CB - "I participate now in choosing my growth. I see where I was limited." UA - "Nope! I don't want to participate at all." LP - "That sounds like hard work and discomfort." WR - "I don't want to change my financial reality." TH - "Yes, I do. Yes, I am ready to lean in and make new choices even if it is uncomfortable."

EB - "No. I don't know where to start." SE - "Of course, I always participate fully." UE - "And also, No. I never participate." UN - "It's not up to me anyway." CH - "God will do it one day. God/Goddess will decide in the end."

CB - "God save me! There's nothing for me to do. There's no point in me trying. It's all predestined!" LP - "I don't actually have free will." WR - "Of course I have free will! What I choose makes a huge difference in the way my life unfolds." TH - "Predestination … What's another word for that? Fate."

EB - "What is my financial fate? What have I been fated to experience?" SE - "I am fated!" UE - "There is no timing, there is only fate. There is no time." UN - "I am fated." CH - "Fated to win!?" CB - "Fated to lose." UA - "Fated to suffer." LP - "Fated to struggle and barely scrape by?" WR - "Fated to come out on top, no matter what?" TH - "Fated to succeed? I vote for that. Can I choose success now?"

EB - "I am open to the possibility of serendipity and synchronicity with money." SE - "I give myself permission to relax and breathe." UE - "I am ready to have my money flows align with grace." UN - "I don't need to know how things will work to be able to have things work out for me." CH- "There's a thought, I am choosing to know that life works for me."

CB - "What if I am provided for." UA - "My financial life is ready to fall into harmony." LP - "I participate with financial grace and harmony." WR - "I am open to receiving good things on a regular basis." TH - "I am available for Divine Timing to dance through my financial reality and show me my path forward."

Deep breath. Wiggle, wiggle, wiggle. Stretch. Look around. Good job! That was a lot to dig up.

Check in with yourself.

Has your SUDS level moved? Do you need to keep going on any one of those tangents about timing, allowance, divinity, or fate before moving on?

Easily Distracted

What are seductions? Technically to be seduced is to be enticed or tempted in a way that will make you change your mind and alter your course of action. What are distractions? Having distraction can be a thing that prevents someone from giving full attention to something or someone else. Aso being in a state of agitation is to be distracted. Temptations, distractions, irritations, seductions - these are all things that pull us away from a target, tangible, ethical or financial.

What would my life be like if I could choose a path forward AND stay connected to the larger vision of that target? How is life changed when I can consistently make progress towards long term targets?

Make a note about current thoughts and feelings and relevant SUDS levels.

KC - "Even though I am frequently distracted from my financial goals, I love and accept myself. I love and accept myself right now. I deeply appreciate all of who I am. I deeply appreciate all of me, even though I am seduced by shiny things. I think, 'that's not my primary target' but it was fun! I get distracted. I've spent money I wasn't planning to spend on things that I don't need. I have these past expenditures and I choose to love myself."

EB - "I've been financially seduced. I've been distracted by 'small' expenditures." SE - "I have been so distracted and off target for a long time." UE - "I have been seduced by short term plans and lost track of long-term plans." UN - "There are so many distractions around me every day." CH - "I am a distraction for other people and other people help to distract me."

CB - "I sometimes seduce people out of their money." UA - "They sometimes seduce me out of my money." LP - "It's a strange thing that we do, teasing and tricking and manipulating money away from each other." WR - "So many financial distractions!" TH - "Financial distraction has been normal. It would be strange to focus and keep my focus for long."

EB - "I don't want to know that I know. It is easier to avoid my capacities." SE - "Yes, I do know that I know." UE - "I like to be confused. I like to be clear headed." UN - "I like to be distracted. I like to be focused." CH - "I like being seduced. It can be fun to be distracted."

CB - "It's so much fun to be off target! Is it boring to be consistent and reliable with money?" UA - "You know what? Maybe my target was someone else's idea about what I should want." LP - "Have I been rebelling against something by being financially irresponsible?" WR - "What am I proving if I make financially rash or risky choices?" TH - "If I love it, I love it! Who's to say it's a distraction? Interesting. What am I committed to creating and experiencing with my money?"

EB - "I was told to absolutely never be this way! My dad/mom told me I could only rely on myself." SE - "I was told to slow down. I was told to act quickly! My mom/dad told me to be careful." UE - "I'm so confused. There is no way to do all the things I was told to do and be with money." UN - "All this financial insanity, distraction and seduction." CH - "What if I could expand and have new options?"

CB - "What if I could allow ease with financial flow to show up for me?" UA - "What if my parents didn't

74

actually know everything about money?" LP - "I could be ready to learn new things that will serve me better moving forward." WR - "I'm going to offer them the benefit of the doubt, and allow that, they did the best they knew how to do for me." TH - "What if I could perceive what is relevant for me financially now? What if I am free to create new outcomes?"

EB - "I am willing to know how to perceive my path forward." SE - "I could be willing to be willing. I open the space now for the possibility that there is a way." Deep breath. UE - "I can perceive and receive what works for me now." UN - "My body is here, telling me, showing me my options." CH - "What works for me in these 10 seconds? Where do I feel pulled to take action?"

CB - "What would it be like to trust my gut instincts and take inspired action?" UA - "What does my body know about being in the right place at the right time?" LP - "What if my body is in tune with amazing resources and possibilities?" WR - "Opening to my innate wisdom could be gentle." TH - "My body is interested in staying alive and having quality experiences."

EB - "I honor myself when I acknowledge the needs of my body." SE - "What if having money is for the benefit of my body?" UE - "Maybe I could ask my body, 'is this a distraction, Or is this a contribution?'" UN - "My body might have valuable information to share with me." CH - "My body has been with me through thick and thin."

CB - "Hi body. I love you. I appreciate you working with me right now. Thank you." UA - "I am ready now, to have a better connection with you, within myself." LP - "I know I've abandoned myself in the past and deferred to other peoples' opinions." WR - "I am sorry. I am willing to learn new ways of being with money that respect my body and support my physical and financial health" TH - "I am ready to open the space for my intuition and heart centered knowing to guide my financial actions.

EB - "What if I could relax around money?" SE - "Wouldn't that be amazing? I'd like to be able to relax about money." UE - "I've been a bundle of stress about money for a long time." UN - "Maybe I can practice taking long, slow, deep breaths and choosing to tap when I feel stress building around financial concerns." CH - "My body could learn to trust tapping to bring me into alignment with my breath." Take a deep breath.

CB - "As I breathe and tap my nervous system is regulated." UA - "When I regulate my nervous system I come out of fight, flight, freeze and fawn stress responses." LP - "Even if it takes some time, practicing EFT, I know that regulating my nervous system would benefit my whole body." WR - "As I learn to breath, tap, and relax, I will connect with my inner resource states." TH - "I love that my body is willing to learn new patterns and that I can choose to alter my experiences around money moving forward."

Take a deep, long, slow inhalation and a long, slow exhalation.

Check in. Do you need water, sugar, salt, movement, sunshine, or something else? How can you support your physical body right now?

Expectation of Limitation

This one is sneaky! Are you defining yourself by the limitations of your past?! There are known and unknown agreements in all of us. Places where we take on rules and regulations -Only, Always and Never patterns that play out in our background noise and quietly 'keep us safe' by limiting exposure to discomfort.

For example, is it inherently dangerous to be seen by a large group of people? What about being heard? Do you have a fear that to be seen, to stand up in front of the crowd, will create the experience of being targeted? Where are we cutting ourselves down, in advance of the possibility of a problem, to preemptively avoid the chance that things will go wrong?

KC - "Oh, I've been defining myself. I've been putting myself in neat little boxes and I have so many labels for who I am and even more for who I am NOT ... And I love that about me. Right now, I love and accept myself even though I've been sorted and organized. I'm all ready to be put in cold storage because I've been so well defined and cataloged! They can put me away on the shelf! They don't need to, I've done it to myself, and I love who I am."

EB - "I've been defining myself." SE - "I have so many collected limitations." UE - "I have prescriptions for how to act. I probably have an expiration date on me somewhere!" UN - "I've been so defined, confined, restricted." CH - "I know all of my limitations so well."

CB - "I bet my list of limitations is bigger than yours." UA - "I bet you're right. I have all these expectations rooted in self-doubt." LP - "I have good

77

reasons for my self-doubt and habits of hesitation!" WR - "I have had bad experiences that taught me well! I know that I have to be cautious and wary with money." TH - "Of course I have expectations of financial abuse."

EB - "I am holding expectations of financial limitation." SE - "I am running my own definitions of financial abuse, seen and unseen." UE - "I am defined! That's normal." UN - "I make myself finite, manageable, accessible." CH - "After all, that's how to fit in!" CB - "If I know who I am then I can be Right. I need to be right about something." UA - "I'd rather be right than risk going after something elusive like happiness or success." LP - " I'd rather be right than happy." Deep breath. WR - "Really? Is that true? Is being right more important than my joy?" TH - "What if these definitions are arbitrary? What if these definitions of myself are confining me and restricting me in unnecessary ways?"

EB - "How would I know if I am capable of more?" SE - "What if none of these things actually defined me?" UE - "What if these inner expectations are limitations? Could they belong to anybody else and not all be mine?" UN - "All things expectations. There are so many of them!" CH - "Oh, these expectations and limitations! I bought them!"

CB - "I've even sold them to other people." UA - "Occasionally I sell limitations. It's like a public service to share limiting beliefs and identities with other people!" LP - "I've helped people to find themselves by identifying their limitations." WR - "After all, people give me labels and the burden of their crap all the time." TH - "For instance, they said that I'm a brat and an idiot."

EB - "I'm stupid, dumb, naive, brilliant, beautiful or dense depending on the day. "SE - "I'm such a hassle! I'm bothering people by asking too many questions." UE - "I have so many colorful labels from the people around me." UN - "Am I a cheapskate or extravagant or both?!" CH - "I am so confused about all these labels."

CB - "These labels don't even all agree with each other." UA - "How can I be a penny pincher and careless at the same time?" LP - "I'm supposed to be frugal and hard working." WR - "But also obedient, brave, polite, dedicated and generous." TH - "I've been trying to figure out all these labels. I have been given so many conflictual identities!"

EB - "Living up to these names and definitions." SE - "Living down to them." UE - "Proving them right." UN - "Proving them wrong." CH - "I have so many labels."

CB - "I love them! I want more labels." UA - "No, I don't! I don't want any of these labels. Make it stop!" LP - "I need these definitions from other people to know who I am." WR - "That's not true. I know who I am." TH - "All these financial expectations, all these financial identities."

EB - "Financial limitations." SE - "Financial projections and expectations." UE - "All this crap about rules and regulations and stipulations." UN - "Don't be seen." CH - "Don't be heard. Shut up. Shut up!"

CB - "But also, speak your mind. Make sure you get heard!" UA - "But keep your damn opinions to yourself! All of these conflicting messages." LP - "There is no universal 'Right way' to be. But there are a lot of ways to be very Wrong." WR - "My best efforts don't seem to add up to much." TH - "I am weary of carrying so much mental and emotional conflictual data."

EB - "Everything I've done to cut myself down in advance to avoid being 'cut down to size' by someone else." SE - "Everywhere I have boxed and labeled and discounted myself." UE - "I anticipate how other people will treat me poorly." UN - "All that that is and has been, I now release it from my body and mind." Take a deep breath and blow it out. CH - "I give full permission for my capacities with money to expand."

CB - "I have full permission to step out of those boxes. I have full permission to step beyond those labels." UA - " I have full permission now to drop all the labels, expectations and limitations known and unknown." LP - "Hi body. Wow, you've been carrying a lot of arbitrary, irrelevant nonsense and trying to make it make sense!" WR - "Thank you for all the years of trying to sort through the financial insanity and chaos we were given." TH - "I am choosing now to release all of that and embrace my own financial reality."

Oh-Kay! Wiggle, wiggle, wiggle, wiggle.

Give yourself a minute to breathe and feel the waves of energy tingling through your circuitry as this information, newly unlabeled and unboxed, is cascading through to impact new aspects inside your system.

Inviting Clarity

We have made a lot of progress. We've been bringing up painful financial topics; where we were holding conflictual data in our bodies, and tapping to release what is not working.

Holding inherited dysfunctional patterns as stagnant reference points means that we project and expect that into the future. That system makes you repeat the behaviors that you wish hadn't happened in the first place!

Today, I would like to go to tapping for calling in the future and allowing for new and different possibilities.

We have some silver coins here to play with. For the purpose of bringing up the energy of money more purposefully, hold a coin or bill. If you can get coins, I invite you to take a little time to roll them around and acquaint yourself with the weight, texture, or sound of it spinning.

Let's start with some general clearing. You can hold on to those as we tap or set it down in front of you.

Notice if you have a starting SUDS level around the idea of new possibilities with money.

KC - "Even though I've been so busy, and money is an ongoing challenge, I am choosing to love myself. I have been preoccupied with living my life and I don't really know yet if all this tapping is going to be enough to change my life, but I can love who I am. I can tell that I feel better when I do remember to tap. I am choosing to deeply and completely love and accept all of me, whether I remember to tap regularly or not. I honor who I am and where I am on my journey. It's all good."

Okay, tapping at the EB - "I've been so busy, too busy to do what I'd like to do." SE - "All this money stuff comes with so many distractions." UE - "I've been having to make adjustments and be present with discomfort." UN - "Money keeps surprising me with ups and downs." CH - "Both coming in and leaving unexpectedly."

CB - "There's so much going on day to day. And it's not just with me." UA - "Financial realities are changing for the whole planet." LP - "Financial upheaval is so uncomfortable." WR - "Financial confusion has become normal." TH - "The way we value everything is changing."

EB - "The way we value ourselves and each other needs to change." SE - "The way we value our time." UE - "The way we value our resources." UN - "All of it is changing." CH - "So much is changing with world currencies." Take a deep breath.

CB - "It is easy to feel lost or overwhelmed." UA - "I'm not in charge of the way things change." LP - "I'm not in charge of the way things are changing around me." WR - "There is so much about the financial world that is beyond my control!" TH - "I can witness what other people are choosing and make choices for myself."

EB - "I can't fully anticipate how these things will impact me." SE - "I don't get to choose how other people will respond." UE - "I see them running old patterns and habits." UN - "They invite me to do that too, but I do not need to join them." CH - 'I have choices to make for myself about my money."

CB - "I can slow down, breathe, tap and choose my reactions." UA - "I can tap when I'm not feeling right." LP - "I can tap for my clarity, and I can tap to pull in new feelings." WR - "I can choose to work through upsetting things and access my resourceful states of mind." TH - "Tapping can help me to get clear and choose what works for my financial well-being."

EB - "I see other people reacting to change with fear." SE - "I see myself and notice where I have been afraid." UE - "I feel the constriction of other people when they panic or focus on what is not working with money." UN - "I feel for myself how my body responds with contraction around financial fear and anxiety." CH - "I am willing now to have a clear sense of how money flows in the world around me."

CB - "I am willing to be in tune with financial possibilities and invite money to flow to me in new ways." UA - "I open space for acknowledging, receiving and perceiving the energy of money." LP - "I'm willing to invite money to be my friend and loving companion." WR - " I'm willing to invite money and to entrain with money so that it flows into my life." TH - "I am willing to entrain to positive outcomes. I'm willing to move with positive financial flows and new beginnings with money."

EB - "There is so much possible now." SE - "I can breathe, tap and participate with the way money is growing." UE - "I choose to participate in creating and generating my financial future." UN - "I am capable of adaptation and healthy growth." CH - "I am willing to participate with my financial growth."

CB - "Things are possible with money now that have never been possible before." UA - "I am willing to be present, aware and inspired with my money." LP - "I am willing to be inspired with my money." WR - "I'm willing to be present and choose what will work for my life." TH - "I can find my stride and adapt with ease around money."

Deep breath. Was there any of that script that stung or really resonated within you? When you do have a positive word or phrase that really stands out, that tells me either that it is very far from what you feel capable of embodying or that you had new space to hear it and to feel how those statements were interacting with your system. Either way, a little more tapping with that vocabulary could help.

Check in. What's your current SUDS level?

Do you have loose ends of negative mind chatter to clean out? Would you like to keep tapping on one or more of those positive statements to find out what else is ready to come online for you?

The Gift of You

What if you are a gift? Who is looking for you? Who is looking to have your services, or even just have your time? Who desires to give you money? Who wants to love you and adore you as a cheerleader?

Do you want to be seen? Do you want to be received? Are you afraid of punishment and unfortunate outcomes if you do show up to be seen or get paid more money?

What would it take to change from the way you have been, to the way you would like to be with money? Let's go ahead and tap for those things. I'm so glad that that's what's up to be moved today.

Tapping on this side of the hand. We always start with the setup phrase when tapping for a new aspect or new topic. KC - "Even though I have all these habits of hesitating and waiting for other people to value me, I now acknowledge and honor myself. Even though I've been hiding and not wanting to be seen, I lovingly accept that about me. I lovingly accept who I am. I have good reasons to hide, and now I'm willing to consider being seen and getting paid. Maybe I'll just be seen by a few people. I'm not sure what's next with my money reality and I love that about me."

EB - "What if I am a gift?" SE - "What if people are looking for me? What if people are happy to see me? UE - "That could be scary. I don't know if it is safe to be seen." UN - "I just noticed an idea, maybe it could be fun to have new experiences with people and money." CH - "New people looking for me for good reasons."

CB - "People hunting me? No. People seek me with good intentions." UA - "How can I know for sure? I can't know for sure if there are nice people looking for me." LP - "There are nice people looking for me? There could be scary people looking for me." WR - "There are people looking for other people for lots of reasons." TH - "I can't tell who is who. Or maybe I can? Do I trust my intuition and my guts?"

EB - "I don't know. I don't know." SE - "Maybe I don't want to know." UE - "I don't want to know what I know." UN - "Yes, I do! I do want to know and perceive how to navigate my finances in healthy and prosperous ways." CH - "Right now the energy of 'No' is bigger."

CB - "The 'No' has been bigger than my 'Yes' has been." UA - "It has felt safer to hide." LP - "It has felt safer to hide. But maybe I am a gift." WR - "Maybe I'm full of magic. And maybe I don't want to share!" TH - "I've been keeping myself separate, 'Just in case' that's better."

EB - "But maybe, there could be people looking for me for joyful reasons?" SE - "Maybe being reached is a good thing sometimes." UE - "It could even be a little bit of fun. How can I know?" UN - "Maybe my body knows the difference. My body does know the difference." CH - "I'm willing to ask my body to lead the way and show me."

CB - "I think my body knows. My body has been with me all along." UA "I think my body has a lot of wisdom." LP - "My body has been learning and growing and changing throughout my life." WR - "My body has a wealth of information about a lot of things that I have not been accessing." TH - "My body has so much information to share with me."

EB - "There are people looking for me and my skills." SE - "I've been looking for me!" UE - "I am a gift." UN - "I choose to appreciate my time and attention. CH - "I bet there are other people who would appreciate my time and attention."

CB - "I do have a lot to contribute." UA - "I have so much to offer and so much I can be paid for too." LP - "There are a lot of people in the world and there's a lot of money changing hands every day." WR - "There could be good people who would be happy to know me and hire me too." TH - "I'm the only one that can give the gift of access to who I am." Take a deep breath.

EB - "I look forward to finding out what I am capable of giving and receiving." SE - "I might want that experience of gifting and receiving large sums of money too." UE - "Oh no. There's that receiving thing again!" UN - "People might be grateful for who I am. They might want to contribute to my life." CH - "No, they won't choose to acknowledge or praise my efforts."

CB - "They're gonna hate me. I've decided in advance. I've decided that no one out there likes me and they can't receive me or afford to pay me." UA - "So I'll just stay home. I'll just stay in." LP - "I'll hide for the rest of my life from what might go wrong and from all that could go right." WR - "Maybe that's unreasonable, but it seems safer to hide." TH - "That's kinda silly. I won't grow very well if I isolate myself. I know that sticking to my comfort zone does not challenge me to grow."

EB - "I do like people sometimes." SE - "I like people who are kind and generative." UE - "I can receive a lot from some people." UN - "I am willing to receive more now than I have ever received in the past." CH - "I am willing to be received, more than I have ever been received."

CB - "I'm willing now to be appreciated. I'm willing now to be acknowledged." UA - "I am willing now to be acknowledged." LP - "People will see me whether or not I participate." WR - "I can choose to help shape the way people think of me." TH - "I will choose to see myself as a gift and inspiration to others."

EB - "I will honor, respect and appreciate myself." SE - "Other people either will or will not honor, respect and appreciate me." UE - "I do. I love, honor, respect and cherish who I am." UN - "Other people might acknowledge and honor who I am." CH - "No. They don't. They won't"

CB - "They never have. They never will" UA - "I won't let them! I won't show up." LP - "They won't get the chance to receive or reject me if I don't cooperate with being seen." Deep breath. WR - "I'd like to be received. I'd like to be appreciated, acknowledged, and respected." TH - "Wouldn't that be amazing to be praised and celebrated as the gift that I am? I could have that outcome."

Check in. Take a few deep breaths. Look around the room. Do you need water, sugar, salt, stretching, wiggling or something else? What SUDS level do you have about being seen or praised?

Looking now at the question of, where have I been separating? What decisions, judgments or conclusions are creating division? Can I now set myself free if I forgive all of me for my part in creating the confusion?

Let's tap. KC - "Oh my goodness! There's so much here. I've been withholding! I've been hoarding my energy and my time. I've been worried I will be rejected, and I accept that that has been true. Even though I have been participating with, and maintaining separation, I now honor and love myself. I see that I've been using judgments and conclusions as a way to keep myself away from other people. I learned really young that it's better to have walls and separation, especially with money! There are secrets that we keep and it's not good to just talk to everybody about everything. I love that I was willing to be just like my family. That is something I chose, consciously and unconsciously. I was very committed to honoring and upholding their rules and right now, I love that about me."

EB - "I've been a scrooge." SE - "I've been hiding myself and hoarding money whenever possible. I've been clinging to it." UE - "I've been hiding things about money. I've been hiding things about myself." UN - "I've been keeping secrets." CH - "I've been hiding my talents and keeping myself secret."

CB - "I've been hoarding my resources, in case there's a bigger calamity later." UA - "I've been taught to be very careful. I've been taught to be cautious." LP - "It might be good to be cautious." WR - "I might be missing chances to connect and to prosper." TH - "I've been taught to expect disaster and suspect the worst from other people."

EB - "I've been taught to be a scrooge." SE - "I've even contributed to making sure other people know to be afraid." UE - "It is appropriate to be afraid with all this monetary chaos." UN - "Money hoarding and hiding myself away is normal." CH - "Being a scrooge."

89

CB - "Screwing other people and screwing myself." UA - "There has been so much that has felt so heavy." LP - "I haven't felt very alive or vital with all of that." WR - "Being careful and cautious can turn into stagnation and festering. Yuck." TH - "I would like to be free again to feel safe and optimistic. I choose to set myself free from self-doubts and fear."

EB - "I'd have to set other people free at the same time to release myself fully." SE - "I see this now. We are stuck in being stuck together." UE - "I acknowledge the lie that has been our financial reality." UN - "I now pardon and set myself, and everyone else, free of these patterns." CH - "I am pardoned and set free in all aspects of my larger Self."

CB - "All of us. None of us. Any of us." UA - "Some of us set free. None of us are free." Deep breath. LP - "I am willing for all of us to be free of this program of financial insanity." WR - "I release the need to get even and get back at anyone about anything." TH - "No, I Don't! Yes, I do. I'm done fighting about money and resources. I am a creator and I set myself free of vengeance."

EB - "I forgive my past." SE - "I forgive others." UE - "I forgive my past confusions and conclusions." UN - "I forgive my future doubts and anxieties." CH - "I forgive my unforgiveness, my secrets and my suspicions."

CB - "I forgive my hesitation and my fears." UA - "I forgive all the confusion that I believed, bought and sold as 'True' about the lies of money." LP - "I release all of these residues from my body." WR - "I forgive all the financial misunderstandings, known and unknown." TH - "I let go of my addiction to stress about money."

EB - "I let go; including the idea that there is anything to forgive or that I've been wrong to be how I was." SE - "There is nothing to forget. There is nothing to forgive" UE - "I did not create the current system of financial dysfunction. I did not create this." UN - "This is not my responsibility to resolve everything for everyone." CH - "I release all of this conflictual content and confusion. Return to Source with consciousness attached."

CB - "There is nothing to forgive." UA - "I am letting go of all the distractions and distortions." LP - "I release all the stories about how I was then, or how I have to be in the future to get money 'the right' way." WR - "There has never been anything That I must forgive." TH - "There has never been, and there still is not, anything or anyone that I have to forgive."

There's a lot of energy on that one. Be still for a moment. Breathe. Notice what's happening with your inner dialogue.

Did you have another thought in your head as we tapped through that round? Was there something that came up for you in that?

Yeah. There is twisting and bastardization in that idea of forgiveness. For most people, as long as you're looking for a way to earn forgiveness, you will be stuck in the loop of it.

If you need to be forgiven, you're locked into a reality where you did something wrong, and there's always going to be something you have to work on in order to fix that feeling of not being enough.

It sours the idea of your future success if you take a broken or faulty version of yourself into creation.

Feeling guilty, ashamed, and wrong keeps you in a little bubble reality that's separate from the wider possibilities of your future. Those last few rounds about forgiveness might be worth revisiting.

Obviously, there are actions taken by cruel or self-serving people that harm others and need to be rectified. That is not what we are addressing here.

Please, feel free to tap more if you need to address thoughts and emotions around your history with the general topics of guilt, shame & forgiveness. These things can be very heavy to carry in our hearts and get in the way of dreaming.

Having the grief of guilt or shame, burdening your mind and heart will cloud your judgment and greatly reduce your ability to function quickly and clearly.

Specifically with financial decisions, continuing to hold shame and guilt about your past may mean that you are open to heightened feelings of self-doubt and susceptible to external emotional manipulation.

Money Has No Opinions

I know it is hard to grasp the shape of a life 'free of financial stress' if that struggle has been everything for you to this point.

Let's tap on the idea of "I have fear and stress around money." Where do you feel that in your body? What's your beginning SUDS level?

KC - "I have witnessed a lot of people in fear around money and finances! I have seen some pretty weird choices made by other people and by myself too. There's a lot of scarcity happening, and I love who I am. I love to Love! Even though I have sometimes felt in the middle of scarcity. I see that now and I love that I'm capable of that. I see that I can be afraid, and I know that means I'm capable of feeling and of changing. I'm capable of choosing. I'm capable and I love that about myself. I can get lost and entrain with the people around me. I can join the pity party. I can be afraid when other people are afraid. I can be anxious. I can be happy, and all the while money is still there. No matter how I'm feeling, I love that about me. I even love that about money. Money is consistent."

EB - "There has been a lot of financial abuse." SE - "I have witnessed. I have participated." UE - "I have even occasionally perpetrated financial abuse. UN - "Abuse of self and others; that is part of this reality." CH - "It has been part of my experience.

CB - "I have witnessed financial abuse." UA - "I have experienced financial abuse." LP - "I know it's there whether I approve of it or not." WR - "I've been taught that financial abuse is normal." TH - "I know that abuse of others is there as an option for many people."

EB - "I have also witnessed financial freedoms." SE - "I have also witnessed great financial ease." UE - "I have witnessed people play with money and enjoy themselves in creative ways." UN - "I have witnessed people burn their money and throw it away." CH - "I've witnessed people die for the promise of money and go to war over resources."

CB - "I've seen a lot of interesting choices made with money." UA - "Some of the choices I like. Some I have approved of." LP - "Some of what I've witnessed I wish I could unsee!" WR - "Many things I disapprove of. I have not liked witnessing those things." TH - "Frivolous, stupid, shameful, irresponsible, dangerous and treacherous things are being done with and for money!"

EB - "Money is still money." SE - "No matter how people treat it. No matter what people choose." UE - "No matter how little or how much someone is willing to have; Money is still money." UN - "What does that mean? What is that?" CH - "What choices do I have without money?"

CB - "What choices do I have with money?" UA - "I've been interacting with money as though it would change something in me." LP - "I have been waiting for an inanimate object to change itself, or to change me." WR - "Isn't money supposed to be a magical solution to everything? I've been waiting for it to change my life." TH - "Well, I can say clearly that that has been disappointing."

EB - "Maybe waiting for money to change my life is not my brightest plan." SE - "But I think I learned that from a lot of other people." UE - "Be angry at money! Blame the lack of money for how I feel!" UN - "Somehow punish money for being absent. Resent money for being too small." CH - "This is interesting. This is maddening!"

CB - "All this monetary weirdness. The personification and villainization of money. As though money has emotion and makes choices on its own." UA - "It's still money. No matter how someone thinks of it." LP - "No matter how someone treats it." WR - "No matter how someone uses or misuses it." TH - "Even if someone destroys money, buries their money in the ground or sets it on fire, the money itself has no opinion. Interesting."

Pause here and breathe slowly for a few minutes.

Yes, we could just go on and on! There's been so much ideology and emotion projected onto currency about what it is and what it isn't ... When having money is good or happy and when it's not okay, somehow sinful, or evil money.

If you have a SUDS level for something specific, please do keep tapping around that aspect to discover your own layers of relief with EFT.

Across the planet we have varied beliefs about how much having money is acceptable and unacceptable. All of those are little rabbit holes. You can keep digging through your thoughts and ideas... There's a point where the digging isn't actually bringing you more of anything new to work on. Notice what your SUDS level tells you.

Revisit the Gamut point technique if your SUDS level is not moving but persists at an uncomfortable level.

After you have acknowledged (processed through unpacking and releasing) a lot of what has been painful for you about financial topics; I invite you to switch over into positive affirmations. If you are ready to embed positive ideas, it will be a bright and graceful experience.

Please note: It is sometimes the beautiful, positive and uplifting ideas that hit core wounds and show us another layer of doubt, grief or anger that needs to be addressed.

For this segment it is helpful to be holding or looking at a coin or bill.

KC - "There money is. I can like it and I can hate it, and I love that about me. Money is there, I can decide that it hates me! I can say that 'this amount validates me!' I can decide if it's my best friend and I love that about me. Money is money. I can have it and I can also not have it. I'm still me and I love that about me!"

EB - "Money is money whether or not I'm around." SE - "I am who I am, with and without money." UE - "I have choices to make." UN - "I have learned a lot about what generates income, and what burns it away." CH - "I can make informed decisions from an emotionally volatile or neutral place." Deep breath.

CB - "I can ask my body for guidance about my financial decisions." UA - "I am willing to remember that my body has also been through everything with me." LP - "I'm going to acknowledge now that my body has also been collecting data from all of my experiences." WR - "My body has also been learning what works and what does not work." TH - "Maybe my body has access to intelligence and wisdom beyond my current understanding."

EB - "In fact, it is possible that my body has been collecting new data from all the people around me for my whole life." SE - "I think my body even carries cellular data from my ancestors." UE - "My body could have lifetimes worth of information to access on my behalf."

UN - "I know that money benefits my body. My body has a vested interest in having enough money to survive." CH - "Money doesn't have an opinion but my body has a vested interest in having money!"

CB - "I can love having money. My body appreciates having good food." UA - "My body appreciates having nice clothing. My body is the one that puts up with my shoes." LP - "My body sleeps in the bed and lives in the house." WR - "Physical things, bought with money are for the benefit of my physical body." TH - "Hi body. Wow. You actually have a very good reason to know a lot about money."

EB - "I wonder, what would it be like to ask my body for assistance here?" SE - "In fact, I am now asking." UE - "Hi body. What would it be like to have more ease with money?" UN - "What is it like to have more ease than I've imagined possible?" CH - "Dear body, I'm sorry. I've been complicating things with my confusion."

CB - "I've been resisting something that could be simple, because it doesn't look like my past experiences with money." UA - "Hi body, I'm willing now. I am asking, would you teach me?" LP - "Would you show me how we can have ease with money." WR - "Show me how to think about money in a way that invites prosperity." TH - "Dear body, I'm ready to experience peace within myself around and with money."

EB - "I choose now to lower my barriers." SE - "I choose to relax and open my perceptions." UE - "I choose to expand my energy and open my heart even with money." UN - "I invite my body to breathe easy, be calmer and more

peaceful as I learn to be connected and open for dialogue."
CH - "Thank you body. I appreciate you."

CB - "Thank you. I love that you're here with me."
UA - "I am willing to experience great things with money."
LP - "I am open to having kindness, gentleness and grace
with money." WR - "I look forward to learning how money
works for me and my body." TH - "Thank you body for
choosing great things and guiding me to actualization."

Okay, take a deep breath. That was kind of long, but
I'm glad we kept going. It really is a big piece of a huge
subject.

This is why I first shared this program over the
course of six months; to give people a chance to build
internal momentum with new habits and integrate the
changes.

This process of tapping isn't just to open the can of
worms and acknowledge, "Well, there's a bunch of painful
crap about money!" But to actually be present with it
gently, patiently, as an invitation to sustainable healing and
growth.

All of this content around releasing the impact of
financial abuse is meant for gradual integration. Checking
in and doing what you can, piece by piece over time.

If you are not ready to move on, maybe revisit a
hard chapter again and tap through the next layers of your
financial content.

But you know, as much as there can be value in
digging and pulling up the past, cleaning out the closets and
witnessing the inherited boogeyman. It is also important to
then swing the other way and be sure that you open the

doors to the flow of wider possibilities and even bigger dreams.

We will need to practice accessing this new space and choosing joy, prosperity and alignment with synchronicity as much as we need practice putting down and ceasing our alignment with the old habits of misery and financial struggle!

Don't just clear out the generational muck and stagnation. Be sure to also receive the resources available to you and plant the seeds for your sustainable financial future.

What Have I Done Well?

In 2017 my facilitator, Christine McIver, asked us to write down '50 things I have done successfully.' At first, I said "What!?! No one has *fifty* things they've done successfully! I know I don't."

Our dear brains, precious and useful as they are, really have been trained to filter for mistakes. Historically it is the deviation from our daily routine that might be dangerous to us. We learn to be very mindful and cautious of errors. A lot of your daily mental processing just fills up with the miscellaneous tracking of everything you think you did wrong. It is neatly filed away for 'in case you need to fix it.' and you know, 'do better next time.' But then that accumulation becomes what feels most important mentally.

When we're hyper focused, fixated on error, we are more likely to create errors. We inadvertently actually drive towards the problem by keeping so many problems in the forefront of our thinking!

So, after spending some time writing down my answers for, "What have I accomplished?" and finding that I did not get nearly to fifty... I started writing mundane things like "I have successfully posted to Facebook. I have successfully loaded the dishwasher. I have successfully washed laundry. I have successfully cleaned my house."

It felt like cheating to write those things, but it got me going in that groove and thinking of successes. It was like doing a Google search. Having my brain finally pull up, "Oh, you want *that* information? You want to know what you've done, right? Oh, you've never asked for that." So, it took me more than a couple minutes to get into it. But

100

then it got easier. I was writing down a whole bunch of silly recent stuff - just from the past year.

I was enjoying the simplicity of "Oh, I did get something done. I did pick up that application and got it all filled out and submitted and it was approved." When my brain said, "Well, do you want anything older than two years ago?" I paused with myself, considering. "Yes. But **What is something from a decade ago that I did successfully?** Maybe there is something I've never acknowledged..."

And that was really a great 'treasure trove' kind of question! There were emotions there that I had never had time to make room for.

Are you allowed to celebrate what you've accomplished? Do you have a SUDS level about being seen and praised for your successes?

Let's do some of that tapping for, "Acknowledgement of success."

Start with the set-up, rubbing the sore spot or tapping the side of the hand. "Even though, in the midst of the chaos that has been my life, I have been focused on my shortcomings and I haven't been focused on my successes, I love and accept myself. Even though I've been so busy, refining myself and trying to get things Right, that I overlooked all sorts of awesome things, I love and accept myself. I choose now to honor and acknowledge myself even though I have not been hearing and receiving praise for what I did get Right along the way."

EB - "There are some things that I did right!" SE - "Even with money, there have been times when I was successful." UE - "Maybe not by someone else's standard of success." UN - "But in my world, I have achieved things." CH - "I have completed tasks and I have reached targets."

CB - "There are things that I have accomplished." UA - "There are things I do every day, and I do a great job." LP - "It's time that I acknowledged that." WR - "I'm good at some things!" TH - "No, I'm not. No. I can't say that. You can't say that. That would be arrogant."

EB - "I've been so busy fitting in and being humble … being worthy…" SE - "I haven't been seen or appreciated and I certainly have not been celebrating what I got Right!" UE - "I got it right? I got it right!" UN - "In fact, I got it right faster than anyone else." CH - "But frequently I back off and doubt myself."

CB - "Self-doubt, so that I fit with everybody else." UA - "That's kind of silly, and really counterproductive." LP - "I did it anyway. I'm so fast. I'm so good." WR - "I can get something accomplished and destroy and uncreate it before other people have even started to notice." TH - "I am magic like that! I have skills and capacities. I have a gift for avoidance."

EB - "I have talents and capacities inside of me." SE - "Sometimes I do know what I'm doing." UE - "I have talents, even with money." UN - "I have capacities with money that I have not used yet." Deep breath. CH - "Is now the time?"

CB - "Body, is now the time? Is it safe?" UA - "Would it work? Would other people approve of me?" LP - "Would I approve of myself?" WR - "I don't care if they approve of me." TH - "Yes, I do. I need to fit in. I need to pay the price of belonging."

EB - "I don't want to fit inside of the rules and regulations." SE - "I have to fit in... Don't I?" UE - "There is safety in numbers." UN - "What?! Safety and numbers? Do I believe that?" CH - "How about safety AND the numbers in my bank account?"

CB - "How about safety and trusting myself?" LP - "How about safety and trusting my intuition about money?" WR - "How about me and my body choosing what works for us on a regular basis?" TH - "It's a little bit like putting a pebble in the pond, and it ripples and ripples, and we see where it goes. I look forward to finding out what comes next for me in this exploration of money."

It's true. We don't always perceive the benefit of a tapping session right away. Sometimes the reverberation carries on for several minutes or imperceptibly for hours and days. A few rounds of tapping with a topic; taking the time to slow down and follow the daisy chaining stream of consciousness through your stray thoughts, will be changing things on many layers of your belief systems all at once.

You can start a session by writing out what's going on for you, gathering SUDS levels and working through those entries methodically. Or you may launch into your tapping with daisy chaining and find out where you land.

I really appreciate groups coming together with a common purpose and working together, going back and forth to process as a team effort. I think we get more aspects of the topic attended to this way. The benefits for group sessions with tapping are a lot different than individual practice.

A group setting helps to accentuate; not just where the problems are, but also that little shifts in understanding and perspective open space for changed consciousness in each person.

Watching someone else work through a related topic lets you 'borrow benefits' as your body integrates the observation of how they moved the energy and returned to balance even with something dysfunctional or painful.

Let's do one more round on trusting yourself, whether or not you feel that that is your topic.

KC - "Sometimes I just know. It's not rooted in my history and not rooted in any conscious data. Sometimes I'm embarrassed about that, and I love that about me. Even though sometimes I ignore my own instincts. Sometimes my team of non-physical helpers is being really loud and clear, and I override them to do something else. Right now, I love that about me. I have all these talents, and half the time I don't bother using them and I even love that about me! I have the freedom of choice and I'm willing to choose what works for me right now."

EB - "Financial chaos." SE - "Form, structure and regulations." UE - "One is better than the other, right?" UN - "I'm not going to tell you which one." CH - "Maybe neither is better than the other all the time."

CB - "Maybe there's another option that no one has discovered yet. And that's okay. Chaos? Yes. Form and structure, or something else completely. What I choose is my choice." UA - "I can be frazzled; I can be scatterbrained!" LP - "I can be focused or unfocused." WR - "I can be zoned out or zoned in." TH - " I can be disassociated and disoriented with money and it's okay."

EB - "I can waste money." SE - "I can waste time and money." UE - "I can save time." UN I can save money. Can I save money?" CH - "I can waste my resources. I can save my resources."

CB - "I have so many options and so many choices." Deep breath UA - "There is a lot going on every day. In fact, I think there's a lot going on with money every night too." LP - "Money changes hands all day every day." WR - "Transactions are happening all around me 24 x 7." TH - "It's all okay. I'm still here, and money is still here. Money is pretty consistent that way. I could choose to be consistent too." Deep breath.

EB - "I have awareness and choice." SE - "I could recreate and reactivate old patterns. I could let go and call for alignment and ease with new outcomes." UE - "I choose to invoke ease with money." UN - " Just like changing the radio station or watching a different movie I change frequencies. I invoke alignment and ease with finances." CH - "I am willing, and I choose over and over again over and over again, as many times as it takes to change my outcomes."

CB - "I know I have that choice. I choose to be aligned and I invoke joy with money." UA - " Oh no! Joy with money is bad isn't it?" LP - "I wouldn't want to be caught having ease, joy or fun with money." WR - "Joy and ease with money would be such an unpopular choice for me." TH - "Joy with money is a judgeable offense!"

EB - "Joy with money can't end well or work well for me." SE - "Oh, wow. If I'm happy things will go badly." UE - "If I'm being happy, I can't be a responsible grown up at the same time." UN - "Bullshit!" CH - "That is bullshit."

CB - "That's such a lie! Being joyous, means I would be irresponsible? No." Breathe. UA - "What is my joy? That is how I connect with money and how it connects with me." LP - "Can I tune into my joyful nature and have even more freedom with money?" WR - "What if the frequency of ease with money could be joyful and expansive for my life?" TH - "I'm willing to find out how much fun and how much joy there is when I am aligned. I choose to integrate the frequencies of money."

Deep breath. Thank you, thank you. So just pay attention a little bit. Whether that's writing it down, posting online, sharing with a group or just kind of observing the internal processing of what you're thinking. And, of course, I hope it's obvious.

If you have little demon critics in your mind kick up and say, "Well! That can't work for me." I invite you to spend a minute tapping on the topic 'This can't work for me.' or 'Things never work for me.' Those are very pertinent to the topic of money, and they are tappable issues.

These are things that you can choose to do to move the energy of the topic. That will help to shift the energy in your body so that it is like choosing a new radio station to listen to.

You'll be on a different frequency, and you'll have a totally different experience - with or without the people around you also choosing that change. Although they are likely to notice that you are behaving differently. They may choose to entrain to your frequency or maybe consciously ask 'What are you doing?' So, thank you. Thank you for leaning into doing this work. I hope that you will have beauty in everything! Until we get together again, be well.

Evaporation and Loss

Does money leave as fast as it comes in? Do you have a SUDS level for this topic? Where do you feel that pattern and the energy of 'Easy come, easy go' in your body?

Begin on the side of the hand. You can hold a coin in one hand and tap with the other or place money on the table in front of you to keep yourself focused.

Sore spot or KC - "Even though I've been having this experience, that money comes and then money goes away before I'm ready, I deeply and completely love and accept all aspects of myself. Even though I've been having this interesting problem with money leaving quickly I choose now to acknowledge all of me. I've been working on this for a while, and I love who I am even when I feel like I should be making better progress."

EB - "Money comes and money leaves." SE - "Sometimes it comes quickly and then I watch it leave quickly too." UE - " Easy come? Or just easy on the way out?" UN - "My expenditures step up to match or even exceed my income." CH - "Here, I thought I was making progress. But then that unexpected bill showed up."

CB - "Isn't that how it goes? Is it 'Easy in and easy out.' or 'hard won and gone too soon.' that's normal?" UA - "Money doesn't seem to want to stay with me very long." LP - "There's always somewhere for money to hurry off to." WR - "Money doesn't stay with me for very long." TH - "I think this is a pattern where a lot of people are stuck running on a loop."

EB - "I have seen so many people struggle with this financial urgency." SE - "I keep seeing myself have this problem too." UE - "I want it to be something that I can change." UN - "I keep looking for 'What did I do wrong?' CH - "Because if I did something wrong, I could change it."

CB - "This pattern of 'hard won and gone too soon' really doesn't work for me." UA - "It's so thick and so heavy to hold onto these patterns." LP - "What is financial stability? What would that be like?" WR - "Money moves so fast. I often feel run ragged trying to keep pace with the bills." TH - "I don't even like to talk about how fast the money leaves my hands." Deep breath.

EB - "Money seeping out every which way." SE - "This 'bleeding money' reality." UE - "It's not fun. It isn't sustainable." UN - "Maybe it's not mine. Maybe it's not mine?!" CH - "I'm really good at running this program of fast paced loss."

CB - "What if I don't have to have money bleed away from me that way anymore?" UA - "What else am I actually capable of choosing and being with my money?" LP - "What capacities do I have with money that I have not yet realized?" WR - "What talents do I have that could come online with money now?" TH - "I think I'd like to focus on that. Thinking of possibilities feels lighter, brighter, and happier."

EB - "Not, 'How do I fix this problem?'" SE - "Where can I create differently? What can I create?" UE - "What can I generate for and as my future with money?" UN - "How can I out create these expenditures?" CH -

"What would it take to change this moving forward? Who can I be? Who can assist me right now?"

CB - "Body? What do you know? What do you know about having and receiving more money and wealth?" UA - "I'm willing now to release all of that old patterning." LP - "I release the residue of that resonance with financial struggle." WR - "I am aware of 'The Rat Race' and I am opting out with grace and ease." TH - "That bastardization of debt wasn't even my creation."

EB - "It's not who I am. I don't need to carry that." SE - "Easy in and easy out. That's an interesting way to be…briefly with, and mostly without money." UE - "Easy in easy out. I can see that pattern running in the world." UN - "Even Steven. It doesn't have to be *my* money story." CH - "Just breaking even. Just barely getting by week to week and month to month."

CB - "Never getting ahead." Breathe.

Feel the sensations in your body. Acknowledge what you've been carrying. Remember, we are bringing these things up to move them out.

UA - "What if this is *my* life to change? This is my life!" LP - "This is *my* financial story." WR - "I can choose to remap and re-write *my* outcomes." TH - "Where could I have more fun with how money flows in *my* life?"

EB - "What am I now capable of perceiving with the flow of money?" SE - "Where can my awareness lead me?" UE - "I am willing now to perceive and access prosperous, expansive and abundant timelines." UN - "I am willing to release the old and receive my new financial patterns with ease. CH - "Body, please show me how to step cleanly into new thought patterns and behaviors."

CB - "Universe, teach me and guide me with grace to alter my financial trajectory." UA - "I'm willing to have my financial reality change in creative and sustainable ways." LP - "My financial reality is shifting in tangible, obvious and subtle ways." WR - "I release all of the habits and addictions that kept me running in the rat race." TH - "I am available for miraculous and serendipitous as well as practical changes in my financial reality."

Okay, take several deep breaths. Maybe get some water and stretch.

Check in. What came up as we went through that? Did you have other thoughts and emotions or remembrances on that topic?

Participant: I had a fear come up when you said that we could "out create our expenditures" like, "Oh, no! How could I do that? I'm not smart enough to do that."

OK. It's true. There are those things that come up while you're tapping. These background noise thoughts are sometimes quick, quiet, and slippery. But these are what become your new topics. Those are the thoughts that you should follow as you tap further.

These skittering pieces of stray thought and vocabulary show us our mind mapping on that subject.

Keep pulling on those threads because they will show you where it's all rooted and tangled up with other subjects or specific events. It doesn't need to make coherent or logical sense to be a related topic and bring you great shifts in your emotional freedom as you keep tapping.

111

Do you have anything else that came up while you did that round?

Participant: Yeah, I thought about "How can money make babies while I sleep!?" Because I keep money under my mattress.

Now that's an interesting thing that a lot of people don't ever think about!

What would it take for this money that I do have to grow? Could my money grow independently to become something that nourishes and nurtures my life; without me always doing the effort and the work? What if money wants to grow itself?

We're gonna keep going a bit more on these thoughts. Rub the sore spot for the set up or tap on the side of the hand, KC - "Even though I have these fears and these irrational thoughts and worries that keep me up at night; right now, I love and accept ALL of who I am. I know right now, in these 10 seconds that I am safe while I am saying these things out loud. I love that part of me that feels free to worry. I have these irrational fears and I love who I am." Okay, tapping through the points.

EB - "My mind spins off on fearful tangents about money." SE - "I have these irrational thoughts." UE - "My mind spins around and around in worry and confusion." UN - "My mind keeps going and going until I am lost and overwhelmed." CH - "I haven't figured out how to have peace with my financial reality yet."

CB - "My brain keeps showing me things I might need to be afraid of. My mind keeps providing anxiety. Just in case that pessimistic future pacing might be useful later."

112

UA - "Just in case. Just in case I didn't remember to be cautious enough. Just in case I was getting a little complacent." LP - "My mind provides me with stress inducing problem scenarios to work through." WR - "I've got plenty of actual events and history to sift through and stew about too." TH - "My brain keeps me on my toes with financial regret, worry and anxiety!

EB - "Sometimes my brain collects current events and tells me about fantastically horrific future timelines." SE - "My brain is very capable of fabricating joy and terror." UE - "Money is just a great heap of a topic to work through." UN - "Money, as a topic, is a wealth of data to sort through and analyze." CH - "All of everyone's experience is there to pick apart."

CB - "All of everyone else's struggle feeds into the material my mind can play with and distort." UA - "I love that about my mind!" LP - "I love my mind, and I hate that I sometimes scare myself." WR - "My mind is resourceful and clever." TH - "My mind is carefully committed to getting everything out of each experience for me."

EB - "I wonder how much I've misunderstood or misidentified regarding my own financial capacities." SE - "How much have I downplayed my capacities for success?" UE -"My mind is creative." UN - "Have I been sorting for 'What's wrong?' instead of 'What is right?' about myself?" CH - "I can see places where I have terrorized myself by latching onto financial fears."

CB - "I know other people sometimes share their fears loudly and in listening to them, I exacerbate my stress levels. They are painting dark ideas as being inevitable." UA - "I've been caught up in stewing and stressing about things I cannot control." LP - "Fixation on a financial problem and rehashing painful details does not foster solutions." WR - "When I feel small, helpless and overwhelmed by the financial trouble around me I do not have good ideas for my future either." TH - "I know that I can shift my focus. Pulling myself away from heaviness is sometimes hard, but I know it is worth doing."

EB - "I love and appreciate my skills, talents and capacities." SE - "I am capable of so many things." UE - "I am willing now. I invite my mind to choose new creations and new financial outcomes." UN - "I invite those aspects of my mind that are financially brilliant to step forward." CH - "That subconscious part of me that has free time to generate a new story about who I am."

CB - "I am willing, and I give permission for my mental resources to feed into the creation of sustainable and accessible prosperity." UA - "I call upon, and I am grateful for, the aspects of me who work to solve that problem." LP - "I also know that I have non-physical teammates who are standing outside of this timeline and loving me through every sort of challenge." WR - "I know I have aspects of myself that have been wounded, fractured and afraid." TH - "Whenever I hear from those fearful voices, (internally and externally) about worry, regret, anxiety and pain..."

EB - "I will lovingly embrace them with kindness." SE - "I choose to remind those aspects that they are welcome to rest now. I can find safety and create safety within my new creations." UE - "I am looking forward to new experiences of safety with money." UN - "Safety with money coming in." CH - "Safety with money staying and accumulating in my accounts."

CB - "Safety with expenditures and bills." UA - "I am open to finding out how calm and peaceful I can be with money." LP - "I choose to focus on the cultivation of peace with money." WR - "When I focus on the generation of my future, I allow all of me to integrate." TH - "Integration of calm, peaceful interactions with money." Deep breath.

EB - "I am planting new seeds for my financial future." SE - "I look forward to cultivating my new outcomes." UE - "There is a journey ahead of me." UN - "I will have many new experiences with money." CH - "I can have safety, peace, calm and clarity with money."

CB - "Safety and trust can grow and expand in my life." UA - "I am open to learning to be peaceful with having money." LP - "I choose to cultivate inner peace with money." WR - "There are people in this world who have wealth and peace. I have my own permission to access that state of being" TH - "I choose the integration of calm, peaceful interactions with money. I will be patient and gentle with myself as I heal and grow into new financial patterns."

Wiggle, wiggle, wiggle. Deep breath.

Check in. What's your current SUDS level?

Are there new topics? Do you have negative mind chatter to clear out? What else is ready to come online for you?

What's Missing?

Participant: So, I feel like I'm missing something with money. I know I'm the creator of my money flows. I am, however, not creating it as fast as I would like to. I feel like I'm missing something. Like there is some kind of piece of the puzzle that I can't see. That if I just knew … 'It'… things would move so much faster."

Kathy: Do you feel like other people have "It" … or is this just something particular to you; missing from your puzzle?

Participant: Well, obviously millionaires have "It." Gazillionaires have it as theirs too. Maybe… I mean, it's like…What do you think I need to do? Do I need to get really clear on my desires?

That's one thing that I've been looking at. Because I would love to have a beach house and what's it going to take to have a beach house? How much money is it going to take to have a beach house? You know? Or is there some other solution? Who would like to have a beach house and give me free use of it? Right? That would be cool.

Kathy: Okay. Let's play with that.

Part of what we do with the tapping; what's happening here, is that we are just talking about a topic to find what feels accurate. So, I'm gonna say whatever words come to mind for me as I'm pulling on that energy, but if there's something that pops in, say that instead and let's follow it. Ok?

Speaking out loud. Rub the sore spot or begin with tapping on the side of the hand. KC - "Here we are, talking about money. You know, there are people who do really well with money. I'm kind of irritated about that, but I also love that about me. I'm really good at observing and comparing. There is a difference between where they appear to be and where I feel like I am. There's all this stuff going on. I have emotional turmoil and inner conflict around money. Having it and not having it. Spending it. Earning it. Receiving it. And I choose now to honor, acknowledge, and love all of me. Even though there's this money stuff happening around me and within me."

EB - "I feel like I'm missing something with money." SE - "I keep missing out." UE - "There's something they must know about how money works." UN - "I wish I knew it too." CH - "I keep going around in circles with money.".

CB - "Getting a bit further ahead and sometimes getting a bit further behind. Sometimes just getting further behind." UA - "I feel like I'm missing something important about money and finances.". LP - "This is confusing for me." WR - "This is frustrating for me." TH - "I am missing vital information for the success of my business."

EB - "There is surely something here I am not receiving." SE - "I think I see other people have this solution that I do not have." UE - "I want a solution." UN - "I think I want their solutions." CH - " I've been seeking for someone else to teach me and show me what works for me." Deep breath.

CB - "I've been desiring to learn what financial secrets they have figured out." UA - "Some of that really sucks." LP - "Sitting with this doubt and fear that I am missing out." WR - "Worrying that I might never know what the wealthy people seem to know about money." TH - "Part of that idea implies that I can't do it on my own."

EB - "I have been desiring their solution." SE - "Maybe this desire has been a way of avoiding my own solutions." UE - "I keep choosing to study with other people about their way of working." UN - " I keep buying another product." CH - "I'm looking for something to come from outside of myself."

CB - "I have been so sure that I don't have what I need. I don't have everything!" UA - "What if I did have all the bits of everything necessary for my life?" LP - "That's ridiculous!" WR - "Why would I hide valuable information from myself?" TH - "What if one part of me does know? What if a part of me can access my path of financial freedom?"

EB - "If part of me knows, that part hasn't told the rest of me!" UE - "I think I should be upset if I've been keeping something this important from myself." UN - "Really, sabotage? I've been stalling myself?" CH - "Maybe true. Maybe not. I might have a good reason."

CB - "But this sucks. I don't think there's a good reason to keep these secrets from myself." UA - "There is no reasonable reason. Should I not be prosperous?" LP - "What reason could I have for holding back from prosperity and abundance?" WR - "Am I holding back? Am I undermining my financial success in any way?" TH - "I'm pretty enough and DARN IT people like me. I even like me most of the time."

EB - "I'm willing now. To lower my barriers and be present with all parts of my Self." SE - "I am willing to entertain the possibility that part of me *does know* my path

118

forward." UE - "I'm willing now to invite that part of me to come through to my surface thoughts." UN - "...To have a new healthy relationship with me." CH - "I am willing to put my barriers down. I am willing now to embrace change and integration in a calm way."

CB - "I am willing now to integrate my past experiences." UA - "I'm willing to have transformation with ease." LP - "I am willing, and choosing to be weirdly happy, calm and peaceful and have money." WR - "I am willing to be unpopular and feel safe, even with making and having money." TH - "I'm willing to have more success and more money than the people around me." Deep breath.

EB - "Is that true? I'm willing to have more than I have ever had." SE - "I am willing to ask for more money than I have ever dreamt possible for myself." UE - "I am willing now. To be whole and to be integrated." UN - "I choose to be potent, capable and to be powerful." CH - "I am willing now to be confident and calm with money."

CB - "Other people are not gonna like these changes in me." UA - "They might think I'm greedy and say that I'm rude." LP - "Rude. Greedy. Selfish." WR - "I don't like to be called names." TH - "They're going to judge me and push me away."

EB - "I've already judged and isolated myself." SE - "I'm better at it than anyone else could be." UE - "I choose to choose something different. I embrace all of myself." UN - "I choose to integrate all of who I am." CH - "I give myself full permission to access all of my financial capacities with grace."

CB - "To have access to all of my resources in an integrated way." UA - "And just for fun. I claim this for myself across all time, space dimensions and realities too." LP - "Am I allowed to do that?" WR - "Maybe. I am willing to find out what ripples through my life when I am the energy of peace and safety with having money." TH - "I am willing to be unusually calm. Unusually peaceful and unusually wealthy."

Participant: Shiver, shiver! I was getting something like... a weirdness about all of that. I think that at some point I swore I wouldn't be rich again!

Kathy: It's up to you. How you would like to process that energy in your system. Tapping for alternate scenarios; concurrent or past lifetimes can be interesting.

I sometimes treat those like the energy of little children showing up with a bedtime story. Obviously, sometimes it's a scary story that I don't want to think about or witness! And sometimes it's a repeat kind of story that is being presented about struggle, betrayal, grief, suffering and even fear of death.

Can you see that? It's like these fearful or wounded aspects come up, and they show you this timeline snippet energy as a story book. If you go, "Oh, you're right! That is terrible!" They will go to put it away again as being 'True' and necessary to keep lurking around.

Versus if you say, "Hi. Come here. Come and sit with me. Let's look through the details for a little bit and allow this content to move and change for us with breathing or tapping. Let's take that story for the entertainment, insanity, or lesson that it is. Receive it. Witness it cover to cover and then, with completion, set it down." Then we have room to ask that aspect of self, "What story would you like to have now?"

Spending a few minutes. To not just dig up the pain or acknowledge what has been running in your background noise; but deeply releasing the alignment with that story as your Truth. Whether that's through some other modality or continuing with EFT to tap through the acupoints and talk.

After you get to clarity and the space of neutrality, keep going into the positive and vibrant place of asking, 'What do I choose to create now?'

I would like you to notice that, even if you have done that kind of visualization before…The most vibrant thing that you could think to imagine, and ask for yourself then, will be different than what you will think to ask for now.

After working through this content for releasing abuses and tapping into financial freedom, you will be changed.

Who you are now is more expansive and your capacity to dream and your willingness to ask is also bigger.

Did that bring up another layer of something?

Check in. Breathe. Stretch.

How can you support your body in this next layer of the system upgrade happening today?

Health, Vitality and Work

Participant: I have noticed that, with my money, I've been getting sick a lot. So, I haven't been able to work my jobs. Okay. I mean, I could be doing a lot better than I am. Because I choose to leave when I'm not feeling well.

I'm wondering, is there a way we can tap for that? Can we get it to stop?

Kathy: I don't know about 'make it stop.' But there are some things there to resolve around the topic of killing yourself for a job.

Does anyone else have a version of that? Or some words that came up as he was sharing? If someone has something- to add another piece, I would include it at the same time.

Participant: Well, being exhausted. That just made me think about how much I need to work with my body and talk to my body. Because when I first started this new job, I knew it was my body that was hired. I know that my physical body is that part of me that requires money.

I just started talking to my body saying, 'Body what would it take for this to be easier for you?' And okay, 'Body, what do you require right now?' and just being really gentle with my body day to day. Whether I was at work or not at work. Does that help?

Kathy: Yes. Thank you. Let's tap for all of those things.

Here again, on the side of the hand. KC - "Even though I've been experiencing a problem I choose to embrace all of me. There are aspects of me that have been struggling and right now I say all of me is good. I lovingly acknowledge all aspects of me, especially because I've been having difficulty.

EB - "I've been struggling..." SE - "having energy... UE - "having health and well-being." UN - "Making money..." CH - "requires time and requires energy."

CB - "There is something here. I have been witnessing a health struggle." UA - "I realize that I've been asking my body to do things that I don't enjoy doing." LP - "Sometimes I push myself to work and it's hard on me." WR - "I have a habit of dragging my body through the day." TH - "There are times when, inside of this reality, self-sacrifice seems to be required."

EB - "The practical part of me recognizes the need to have this job." SE - "There are other parts of me that would rather stay in bed." UE - "And that part of me has been getting my body to slow down, stay in bed and go back to bed." UN - "I see this pattern. It can be useful sometimes to rest." CH - "I adore that I have this capacity to go back to sleep."

CB - "I know it works the other way around too." UA - " I can recover instantaneously when there's something fun to do." LP - "When I'm inspired, I can access astonishing reserves of energy." WR - "When I am uninspired, I can be incredibly lethargic and even melancholy." TH - "I love that about me." Deep breath.

EB - "I love who I am." SE - "It's true. I need to work." UE - "No, it's not true." UN - "Yes, I do have to trade my hours for dollars, whether I feel good or not." CH - "No? Is there another option? I don't know."

CB - "I have to go to work. I have to put in that many hours each week." UA - "I have to pay the bills. LP - "At least that has been true." WR - "I think working and working hard is the way it has to be." TH - "No. Maybe I don't have to. Yes. I do believe that I must work, in some way."

EB - "Yes. I will always have to work hard to have income." SE - "No. I won't. I don't want that to be true." UE - "All of this conflict does not feel good in my body." UN - "I honor how I feel." CH - "I choose to witness all of this. I've been feeling inner conflict about my job." Deep breath.

CB - "All of these points of view are valid." UA - "There are many ways to look at the same situation." LP - "What works 'well enough' right now, may not work later." WR - "What worked for me in the past may or may not work in the future." TH - "I choose now to allow my inner dialogues to resolve peacefully."

EB - "I'm willing to hear, and perceive clearly…" SE - "what is actually relevant and required for providing my quality life?" UE - "What is actually possible?" UN - "I am willing to embrace all of who I am." CH - "I am willing to honor all aspects of myself."

CB - "I am frequently unreasonable. I push both ways - in wanting to play and requiring myself to work." UA - "I have been unreasonable in an unreasonable environment." LP - "I have talked to the people around me and they are unreasonable too." WR - "They have taught me to be unreasonable." TH - "I have a lot of practice demanding irrational things from myself."

EB - "I'm doing a really good job." SE - "I'm doing really well with being unreasonable." UE - "I have learned to duplicate this conflictual reality." UN - " I'm having so much fun with the insanity!" CH - "No, I'm not enjoying working myself to sickness!" Deep breath.

CB - "Ok. It actually is not any fun, even if they pay me well. This is hard." UA - "I wonder, what would my life look like..." LP - "if I could relax and choose something sustainable?" WR - "How could my working change to better match and support my healthy physiology?" TH - "What would my life feel like to be congruent with gentle income?"

EB - "What does my body know about drawing in more money?" SE - "What does my body know about the creation of my reality?" UE - "I am willing to create my reality in new and healthy ways." UN - "I am willing now, and in fact I choose to instigate..." CH - "the required changes to have my desired reality be the dominant outcome."

CB - "I am willing to be the dominant presence and voice of authority." UA - "No, I'm really not." LP - "That would be hard work. It's too scary to assert myself and change things." WR - "I'm not up to that kind of a challenge." TH - "Yes. I could change things for the better."

EB - "If you make me really uncomfortable, then I will get mad and change everything!" SE - "Or maybe, if you tell me 'I can't take care of myself,' then I will!" UE - "I've got to prove something to somebody!" UN - "I need an audience or a good opponent before I will put in that

125

much effort." CH - "It's too hard to choose a healthy life. Who wants 'more luxurious' or 'easier'?"

CB - "What would I even do with stamina or 'more grace' in my daily life?" UA - "You can't make me do it!" LP - "Maybe I'm just acclimated to struggle and hard work." WR - "Maybe I'd be bored with my life if I worked at a job that wasn't so demanding." TH - "Pushing through exhaustion and overriding my body is just the adult thing to do, isn't it?"

Take a deep breath. Check in. Stretch.

Integration of Aspects

Participant: I'd like to get up and go run around in a forest! Thinking, tapping for all this stuff about how I have had to be when I'm at work… I remembered that I feel better outside when I choose to expand out and imagine I can pull from the earth and the trees. It helps even to just imagine it when I can't be on the mountain."

Kathy: Does that imagery help you be in continuous circulation of energy while you're working, instead of just flowing to them? Like providing the service from your own reserves versus being in communion and being nurtured and sustained by the earth at the same time?

Participant: Yeah. I like the idea that I can be sustained and nurtured even while working. I don't want to call it work... Yeah. I liked when you said, 'provide a service.'

Kathy: There's an interesting thing. You might dig more into, or play with, listening to what wording are you using right now? How do you feel when you say job? Where could you tweak that languaging, even a little bit?

Sometimes when there's a long list of things that have to happen, and I need the playful, hedonistic child aspect of myself to be on board with making it happen, I rephrase and reframe a little bit.

It helps to take the view of what you're doing and shift it to include something about the positive outcome. Be sure to focus on what will get accomplished, like, 'We're doing this work now so that we can go on that fun trip next month.'

Then with that included as the focus, more of your being can participate in the joyful, generative creation of the future; instead of just tripping on the small picture. It's hard to feel inspired with 'I just have to do this or lose my job and then my whole life falls apart.'

Okay? There's the short-term focus versus a larger, long-term focus. And the more time you can spend, present, congruent in that larger focus; the more likely you are to actually have those little glimmers of insight and inspiration that really show you where you could be altering your path.

Participant: Something that was up for me. It feels like I've been 'spinning my wheels.' I think I keep working to 'look busy' but not really being productive. I'm not sure why. I don't create what I'd like to get done .. what I think I could be doing. You know?

Kathy: Yep. I've done that too. Let's tap.

Rub the sore spot or start on the side of the hand. KC - "Even though I've been struggling to solve something that doesn't need to be solved, I love that about me. Even though I've been working hard to polish surfaces and tie up loose ends … that don't *actually* need to be attended to... I completely accept and love myself. I've been making busy-work for myself! I've been using my resources to stall, and I love that I'm capable of that."

EB - "That's soooo cute. I hate it!" SE - "I'm avoiding something." UE - "The next phase of my creation is waiting." UN - "Maybe it is bigger than I want it to be... That's uncomfortable." CH - "I've been trying to figure out how to slow things down."

128

CB - "I've been using my time to look productive." UA - "I've been doing lots of things to appear on task." LP - "There's an endless supply of things that could be tended to." WR - "There is a difference though, between busy - work and productive work." TH - "I've kept busy without actually making much progress."

EB - " I am so capable. I want more progress." SE - "I like what I do." UE - "Sometimes I show up and shine." UN - "Sometimes, I dally. It's easy to be distracted." CH - "I have all these skills and so many capacities."

CB - "But I keep giving myself away as I spend time on what doesn't really matter." UA - "I'm wanting myself to honor and value my time and energy." LP - "When I'm willing to waste my time, other people show up and waste it too." WR - "It's all pretty silly. I have this grand vision, but I'm not taking the necessary actions." TH - "I know how this works."

EB - "I know there's a place inside where I do know what's next and I am very clear." SE - "I do remember to breathe myself into centered calm." UE - "I don't really have a good reason to procrastinate." UN - "Procrastination. Avoidance is just a habit to have." CH - "I've gotten really good at it, but I don't actually have a good reason for stalling."

CB - "That's interesting. If I really don't have a good reason, maybe I have a choice to make." UA - "I choose to breathe and tap through whatever arises." LP - "I choose now to acknowledge..." WR - "everything I have been doing that works well and ..." TH - "everything I have been doing that actually does not serve me." Deep breath.

EB - "I acknowledge the places I have been hesitating." SE - "There are places I have been robbing the world of my gifts by playing small." UE - "I'm pretending to be less than who I am." UN - "What's right about pretending?" CH - "As though with pretending I can be other than who I am." Deep breath.

CB - "I acknowledge where I was." UA - "I choose to release that hesitation and procrastination." LP - "It is a choice. I see where I was." WR - "I acknowledge that, and I honor what was true for me." TH - "I can choose to show up as more of who I am and to share my gifts."

EB - "I can even choose to be paid for my work." SE - "I choose to be paid." UE - "I can choose to work with respectful, paying clients." UN - "I require financial compensation for my work." CH - "I have the demand for this change arising in my universe."

CB - "I require an increase in my financial wealth." UA - " I require this change." LP - "I invite my transformation to unfold with ease, joy and glory." WR - "I open the space to participate with graceful changes." TH - "My body is ready to have the ease of grace in my work." Deep breath Wow.

Thank you for tapping through all of that! Thank you for wondering what else is possible for your life.

I hope you will keep going. Check in.

Do you have a residual SUDS level about procrastination, or a different aspect of the last few rounds?

Anticipation of Financial Stress

Let's start with some general tapping, just on the topic of miscellaneous money stuff and see where we go.

Tapping on the side of the hand. KC - "Even though there's still all this money stuff and it feels bigger than I feel ... I choose now to accept all of me. There's a lot going on and I love who I am. The world has a lot of struggle with money. I have had a lot of struggle with money. I've been having some interesting things with money, and I love who I am."

EB - "I've been witnessing a lot of weird stuff happening with money." SE - "The world just seems to get crazier and more treacherous." UE - "Here I am, working to straighten myself out and the world gets more complicated." UN - "I've been working on this money stuff for a while. When will it change?" CH - "I would like my money situation to just be different already!"

CB - "Shouldn't it be different by now? Like really different in a big way?" UA - "What about change for the whole world?" LP - "I would hope that everyone, everywhere wants a better life." WR - "Don't we all need similar things and have similar desires?" TH - "Don't we live on an amazing planet with an abundance of resources?"

EB - "Don't we have all the information to be able to change this? SE - "Are we not capable? Are we not willing to change? UE - "I think we ought to be capable of solving lack and hardship for humanity." UN - "It looks so doable from where I'm standing." CH - "But financial reality on the planet frequently feels like an insane mess." Deep breath.

CB - "I frequently feel inadequate." UA - "I've been feeling not up to the task of changing my money when there is so much dysfunction around me.". LP - "How can I be calm and collected with the world going nuts?" WR - "Isn't that dangerous to be detached and independent of what everyone else is choosing?" TH - " I've been struggling with all of these things."

EB - "I know that the insanity around me isn't mine." SE - "Have I just been witnessing struggle?" UE - "Have I seen anyone thriving right now?" UN - "I have so much awareness every day." CH - "I would like to have more clarity and ease with my financial awareness."

CB - "I choose to allow more ease in my perceptions." UA - "I choose to have more allowance for what I am aware of." LP - "I choose to have allowance for how I am feeling." WR - "I choose to focus on what is working for my life." TH - "I choose to have more allowance for how I am thinking and feeling."

EB - "I even choose to have more allowance for other people and their actions." SE - "I can be aware of them and remain peaceful." UE - "I can be aware of their struggle, and I can have allowance for what they choose." UN - "What would it be like to let go?" CH - "What would it take to have my financial independence?

CB - "I am willing to find out what it is to feel allowance for all of this financial stress." UA - "I choose to have allowance for myself about my situation." LP - "I can witness the world around me and choose my path forward from a place of awareness." WR - "My ongoing connection to my source keeps me open to healthy adaptations." TH - "Financial stress could be a thing of my past."

Breath. Wiggle, wiggle.

Participant: There was something in there for me that has been feeling really heavy, though it did shift some.

Kathy: As with all of this, you would check in on 'How is it feeling now?' Do you need to go back and do more on that particular topic? Or did it bring up something else that is the more vital and relevant topic?

Participant: I'm at a point where I say okay, well, 'I'm gonna do this.' But then, if I choose that I worry I won't have the funds, or the way to do something else in the future if I spend my money now.

Kathy: Okay. Let's tap on that. Sore spot or starting on the side of the hand.

KC – "Even though… Even though I have a suspicion that if I spend money now I won't have money to spend later, I deeply and completely love, honor and accept all of myself. There's a part of me that is worried, and sometimes panicked about money, and I love all of me. I choose now to lovingly embrace all aspects of myself, even though sometimes I worry and sometimes I stress about money." Deep breath. Tapping through the points.

EB - "I am concerned about my future." SE - "my past tells me that sometimes finances don't go so well." UE - "I have stress in my body about money." UN - "I have what I think is a valid concern about money." CH - "I have witnessed many people have this problem. They spend money excessively and then later have the experience of lack."

CB - "I have a valid concern." UA - "I have a valid reason to hesitate." LP - "I have been feeling afraid and

133

hesitating." WR - "I don't want to make the wrong choices and suffer later." TH - "Sometimes I let that hesitation and concern stop me from taking action."

EB - "Maybe that's a good way to be." SE - "Maybe it isn't." UE - "My concern may be rooted in the past." UN - "My concern may be rooted in current awareness." CH - "I wonder. What is the difference?"

CB - "I wonder how I could tell the difference?" UA - "I think my system knows the difference." LP - "My system knows the difference whether the data is coming from the past or from my awareness and intuition." WR - "I do have awareness and intuition around financial matters." TH - " There are times when it is right to hesitate. Sometimes I don't have all the information yet, and I am happy to wait. I am happy to wait and make a choice that serves me better later." Deep breath.

EB - "There are other times when hesitation actually costs me money." SE - "There are times when waiting means I have missed the chance. UE - "I don't like missing opportunities or wasting money." UN - "I don't like hesitation and missing out. CH - "So much doubt about money."

CB - "All this doubt swirling around inside of me." Deep breath. UA - "When I doubt myself, I disregard my own knowledge." LP - "It doesn't feel good to doubt myself." WR - "I don't like always looking outside of myself for instructions." TH - "I've been taught to doubt myself."

EB - "What if I do know what feels light and bright for my body?" SE - "What if my body is telling me with the sensations of light and heavy?" UE - "I am willing to have clear communications with my body." UN - "I am willing to trust my body." CH - "I've been watching other people doubt themselves and doubting their capacities."

CB - "I've been seeing them doubt me and my capacities too." UA - "I have learned to doubt myself." LP - "I have learned to doubt other people." WR - "I doubt them, but I doubt myself even more." TH - "I am in the habit of second and third guessing myself." Deep breath.

EB - "What if I know more than I like to admit?" SE - "What if I know what would work for me?" UE - "What if I can have my awareness and trust it too?" UN - "I am willing now to ask more questions about money and finances." CH - "I recognize that I am not who I was. And I am not like other people."

CB - " I know that I am capable of generating and creating change. I know that I have choices." SE - "I know that I have a variety of options." UA - "It's true. Sometimes there are big events!" LP - "There are mass consciousness, collective events." WR - "There are things beyond my control that will impact my money." TH - "Whatever else changes around me, I can have myself and my capacities on my side."

EB - "I am resourceful and inspired." SE - "I am resilient and tenacious when necessary." UE - "I have me! And I am worth having." UN - "I choose to trust myself and my awareness." CH - "I choose to know what I know about how money works in my life."

CB - " I choose to choose for myself; knowing that I can choose again." UA - "My life is mine to change." LP - "I choose to trust myself to grow in healthy ways." WR - "I am self-referencing about financial concerns." TH - "I know how to accept guidance and ask for help, when necessary, but I know that I am capable of navigating my life." Deep breath.

So come back to the room. Look around. Blink, blink, blink. Stretch.

Kathy: Did we get to the pieces of it, or was there another part?

Participant: We got a lot of pieces. I still have some inner conflict and the feeling that I need to be hesitating. I'm still wondering if I will have enough.

Kathy: Do you own your body? We got to that a little bit in the last round. But the continuation here is having gratitude for family *and* being wherever you are.

Gratitude for all of those situations that have given us experience and given us strength... Having gratitude for the challenges of our lives; for what we have learned from our past, and gratitude for the people who are around us who 'do struggle' as a way of life.

They show us and teach us things, so that we don't have to play out that scenario on ourselves to see it happen.

You watch them and you get to know how that works. You can hold gratitude for your capacity to choose something unlike what they are creating.

Let's do a little bit more on that. Beginning on the sore spot or on the side of the hand. We're going to start with a new setup phrase.

KC - "Even though there's still a lot going on in the world, and I'd like to have more money... I choose now to love and accept myself. Even though there's so much that I have experienced, and there's so much I have not wanted to experience, I love and accept all of me. Even though there are parts of my financial history that I wish hadn't gone that way... I love who I am."

EB - "My financial past is full of interesting textures." SE - "There are things I like and things I don't like about my financial history." UE - "There are people I love. There are people I resent." UN - "There are places where I have been joyful." CH - "There are places where I was sad."

CB - "There were times where I have been angry and full of rage about money." UA - "I perceive my financial timeline. It is full of so many people, places and events." LP - "I really don't like some of what's on the timeline." WR - "I do like some of it. There have been good times with my money." TH - " I am willing to see that there is value in all the different textures of emotional experience that I have had with money."

EB - "I am willing to admit that there was value in the good stuff and there was value in the bad stuff." SE - "I know I have been impacted." UE - "I have been altered by good people and bad people." UN - "In fact, I know I would not be who I am without all of those things. CH - "There is an essence of me, that has always been and will always be, and I am shaped by my experiences too."

CB - "Sometimes I've had money to play with." UA - "Sometimes I've had a lack of money to play with." LP - "Having no spare money to work with is frustrating." WR - "Needing to hustle all the time is exhausting." TH - "Things are much easier with money in my life."

EB - "Things can be rough with or without money." SE - "Things can be easy with or without money." UE - "There are people who help me. There are people who hurt me." UN - "I have experienced all of these things with and without money." CH - "I choose now to be grateful for all of the money that has come to me."

CB - "I am grateful for who I am with or without money." UA - "There are events for which I'm really grateful that they have ended." LP - "There are events I wish I could go back to and enjoy again.
WR - "It wasn't all bad or all good." TH - "For some of it I'm really glad I don't have to see those people anymore! And there are other people that I miss."

EB - "For some of it I'm sad that I don't see those people anymore." SE - "I celebrate some of my past because it ended." UE - "Right now I am grateful." UN - "I choose to be grateful." CH - "I have that choice."

CB - "It's one of my capacities to choose how I feel. To choose how I will react."

UA - "I choose how I remember and whom I remember." LP - "I choose what I keep alive in my mind." WR - "I choose what I speak. I choose when I speak" TH - "I speak gratitude. I choose to remember the things that worked and the people who helped me succeed."

EB - "I choose to ask questions day to day." SE - "How can my money work for me today?" UE - "I choose to say Yes! Thank you. and more please?" UN - "I have gratitude and I'm so grateful for so many things! CH - "I'm even grateful for who I am."

CB - "I am grateful for my life." UA - "I am grateful for possibilities." LP - "I am grateful for kind people." WR - "I am grateful for time to rest and integrate change." TH - "I appreciate the time to reassess and adapt to my shifting financial reality."

Deep breaths. Wiggle, wiggle and stretch. Get water if you need it.

That was kind of nice. Did any of that bring up something more specific about your money history? Check your SUDS level about anticipating financial stress, or future hardships.

Attuned to Struggle

Participant: My past keeps repeating. I feel that my past forces my future into a particular shape. I have family fears, and obligations that limit what choices I can make with my money.

Kathy: Thank you. That's a good aspect of money worries to get to. It's a really common impediment to feeling your financial freedom. Let's go ahead and start on this side of the hand again.

KC - "I love who I am. Even though, no matter what I choose, I'm still part of my family. I love who I am even though I have a financial past. I think that that will shape my future and I love all of me. Even though I have witnessed my family's financial patterns repeating themselves in my life, I love and accept who I am."

EB - "These are causal incarcerations." SE - "I am bound by known and unknown, old financial habits and patterns." UE - "I'm bound here. I am going to repeat the same mistakes my parents made." UN - "I learned really well, how to be the same kind of 'messed up' that the rest of my family has been." CH - "It was part of my daily life and unconscious imprinting."

CB - "They taught me about money. They taught me to have confusion and dysfunction with money." UA - "They taught me financial stupidity, right along with teaching me to walk and talk, eat and dress myself." LP - "Right along with teaching me to speak, they showed me poor money habits." WR - "My inherited family patterns are a mess." TH - "I have so much financial dysfunction accumulated." Deep breath.

140

EB - "I've just been handed a bunch of family fears." SE - "I have inherited family oaths," UE - "There are named and unnamed family obligations and commitments." UN - "Then there is the issue of family loyalty." CH - "I better be just like them and do everything that they do with their money too."

CB - "Obviously, it would be rude to choose something different for my money." UA - "They will be embarrassed if I step outside of their normal parameters." LP - "I will be embarrassed if I start to show up differently with my monetary priorities." WR - "Is it better to conform and just be comfortably uncomfortable doing what they think is best for me and my money?" TH - "Does it make them look bad if I change things? Will they feel bad if I don't struggle the way they have struggled with money?" Deep breath.

EB - "Do I have to prove that I love them by following their financial patterns in my life?" SE - Do I have to demonstrate my loyalty by suffering?" UE - Do I have to demonstrate my belonging to the group by buying and using the same financial hardships that they experience?" UN - "Must I 'fight the same fight' and use the same patterns that they use?" CH - "Am I bound? How does that financially help anyone?"

CB - "I've been experiencing the same problems." UA - "I have been struggling with my money." LP - "I can witness that I'm doing what the people around me are doing." WR - "But do I really have a choice?" TH - "Is financial struggle really a pattern that I can change?" Deep breath.

EB - "There are people who tell me I can have something different happen with my money flows." SE - "I have a suspicion that financial change is possible." UE - "I'm choosing that: It is possible to change my reality with money." UN -"I think I can change my financial story and have better outcomes." CH - "I think I can change my financial reality." Deep breath.

CB - "What if my financial reality could be mine?" UA -"They have a well-established financial reality and following them really hasn't worked for me." LP - "It has not even served them reliably." WR - "Maybe, they did the best they could do in each circumstance. Maybe I am doing my best too." TH - "I am aware of so much and so many possibilities. There are places where I can learn new patterns and new habits with money." Deep breath.

EB - "There are things I can do to gracefully institute and maintain new patterns with my money." SE - "Tapping is one of the things I can do to help my body and my being find healthy changes." UE -"Meditation is something I can do to change my thoughts and feelings." UN - "There are even certified financial and career counselors that I could talk to about my options." CH -"I could do this, I can't do this." Deep breath

CB - "I'm willing now to choose the creation of something that works for me." UA - "I can love my family and walk away from their unhealthy financial patterns." LP - "I can be loyal to my family and create something new." WR - "I can love my family and choose something different for my money." TH - "I love my family and I can love myself at the same time." Deep breath.

EB - "I see what I've been doing with my finances. I see what they've been doing with their finances." SE - "I see new possibilities for them and for myself." UE - "I am willing to choose to create even if they do not change anything." UN - "They might even get mad at me... My changes might scare them." CH - " they might feel attacked. They might feel abandoned." Deep breath.

CB - "They might be angry." UA - "There might be tears, or frustration as I change." LP - "I'm willing to find out what else is possible for my generative financial future." WR - "What else is possible? There might be joy! There might be happiness." TH - "It may take persistence and some effort to change my habits, but I'm willing to find out what new things I can create with my financial brilliance." Take a deep breath.

Check in with your body. Wiggle, wiggle, wiggle and stretch.

Okay. That was actually quite a lot of content. It was a pretty dense batch to tap through.

I think that this section is going to be one that bears repeating on another day. If you come back, to go through to tap again in a week or so, you will benefit in new ways.

Even if you tap with exactly the same script, following the same prompts, it will hit slightly different threads and aspects of your topic will be accessible... There will be different energy patterns in your system that will say, "Oh, I couldn't move last week, but I can move now." And kind of like renovating a house and changing paint or carpet... There are layers and layers of things that have built up around each topic. Sometimes a round of tapping to address one subject is effective just for that specific layer. Frequently, a round of tapping will cause a cascade and pulling one-layer hits other aspects all at once.

We can't always identify and start with the deepest, earliest, or most painful event.

If an old event has shaped our personality, our bodies won't allow instant and vulnerable access to the deepest problems.

We get to work our way there, layer by layer building trust and respect with our mind-body system so that we do not have a 'belief system crash' and fall into depression or a painfully fractured emotional state.

By initiating a system rebalancing, Emotional Freedom Techniques are beautifully suited to work with your system to gently unwind very complicated problems without causing inadvertent damage.

The more patiently and gently you're willing to be with your application of EFT, the more gracefully things unwind. Change can happen quickly with a gentle approach as your body learns to trust you.

Money Madness

Before we begin, it does help to assess your discomfort. So, zero to 10, How big is anger for me around money? How much shame am I holding about money? Is this just a little irritation that bothers me sometimes? Or is it an enormous stress that keeps me up at night or sends me into a panic?

You'll want to actually identify that SUDS level for many different related aspects because 'everything about anger with money' is a conglomeration of a lot of things. And that's where a lot of people just kind of walk away and consign themselves to misery, because it seems too big to tackle.

When, if you took the time to look into each of those events, you could address each one of them and unwind the emotional discontent.

Let's start with something generic and then check in again.

Tapping through the points and talking out loud is valuable even if you don't believe the positive statements at 100%. Tapping while you say things will help to move that energy of doubt and any unnamed or unconscious related content too.

On the side of the hand.

KC - "Even though I'm stressed about money right now, I also love and accept myself. These things are stressful, and I have valid reasons to be worried … And I love who I am. I love all of me. I totally accept every aspect of who I am even though there are money worries right now."

145

EB - "Money is stressful." SE - "Money stress." UE - "Money worries." UN - "I have things to worry about with money." CH - "There are bills due very soon."

CB - "It is reasonable that I would be stressed about this." UA - "These are stressful things." LP - "Money worry" WR - "Money stress." TH - "There is so much to worry about with finances."

EB - "Money going out." SE - "Money coming in. UE - "Mostly money going out." UN - "This pattern is not working for me." CH - "Money stress."

CB - "I have so much worry!" UA - "There's more worry than money in my life." LP - "I'm really good at worrying." WR - "I'd like to be good with money." TH - "I have an ability to worry. But I do not love that."

EB - "I have a capacity to stress." SE - "I've been demonstrating that I'm really good at worrying." UE - "I wish someone would pay me to worry. Haha!" UN - "I'd be good at it." CH - "I wouldn't like that job. But I am good at this job."

CB - "There are things I am good at." UA - "And money has room for growth. Deep breath, LP - "I could grow in terms of my knowledge of financial concepts." WR - "I could grow my levels of comfort and confidence with money." TH - "I recognize that people have not taught me appropriately how to be confident with money."

EB - "I've actually learned a lot of bad habits." SE - "There have been a lot of bad habits in the people around me." UE - "People around me have taught me bad habits with money." UN - "It's not money's fault that I have had difficulty." CH - "It's not my fault that I was given faulty information."

CB - "There were a lot of dysfunctional things about money in my home." UA - "There are a lot of dysfunctional things about money in the country." LP - "and financial problems in the world and in the world." WR - "Money has been a mess for a long time." TH - " It's bigger than I am."

EB - "The money madness -it's not all mine." SE - "I am not responsible for the whole of the problem." UE - "I can open space to resolve my portion and my habits." UN - "I don't need to solve the larger money problems. CH - "I am aware of a lot of problems with money."

CB - "Money madness. I have felt it." UA - "I have witnessed it. I don't have to solve it." LP - "It is enough to work on the issues of my own life." WR - "I am responsible for what I choose to do with my own time, energy and resources." TH - "I don't intentionally cause financial problems and I get to choose what I will create with my money moving forward."

Check in. Was any of that larger, like it had a bigger zing to it?

Participant: Yes. It was that I really did learn bad habits from my family. I'm bothered by that right now.

Kathy: Okay. So now that becomes our new topic. We're gonna go back to the side of the hand because we are changing topics.

KC - "People who love me taught me bad money habits and I love who I am. I fully appreciate who I am and I'm mad that I've been taught dysfunctional money patterns. I see this here; this anger about money, and I love who I am. I fully embrace all of this, even knowing I have learned bad habits."

EB - "Bad habits." SE - "I learned about financial ruin." UE - "Financial dysfunction." UN - "Hoarding. Scarcity and fear." CH - "Overspending."

CB - "Running away." UA - "There are so many bad habits." LP - "There are so many versions of how to avoid money." WR - "Craziness, anger and chaos with money." TH - "All these people are crazy with money!"

EB - "I've been taught bad habits." SE - "Before I could even talk!" UE - "Before I could walk." UN - "My parents were running all these financial programs that didn't work for them either!" CH - "My body learned to mimic dysfunction with money."

CB - "Wow. Hi body. I love and appreciate that you've been duplicating what you thought was the only way to be with money." UA - "I choose to love that about you." LP - "I appreciate the capacity I have to duplicate other people's realities." WR - "Dear body, right now I open space for new possibilities." TH - "We have all of this dysfunction running our money, but it's not mine. It's not yours. It predates all of us."

EB - "Instead of trying to solve it for the world," SE - "I open a little bit of space in my world; in my life and my body for a new financial pattern." UE - "I wonder what it could be like to release what isn't mine?" UN - "I think it could be brilliant." CH - "Body, I wonder what you know about having ease with money."

148

CB - "What about having ease with income?" UA - "Dear body, I think you're brilliant." LP - "I haven't been asking you." WR - "We've just been running these old patterns." TH - "Oops. Dear body, I would like you to guide me now in creating new financial outcomes."

EB - "I am willing for you to teach me, what you know about brilliance with financial freedom." SE - "I suspect that you've been gathering data for decades." UE - "You've been witnessing and collecting all of it from everyone." UN - "I'm ready now. I'm ready to receive the distillation and the essence of our financial brilliance." CH - "Body, what works for you?"

CB - "I think you have a great sense for what will generate our future." UA - "Body, I think you know which steps to take." LP - "I'm willing for you to guide me with ease and financial grace now." WR - "I'm willing to have communion with myself around finances." TH - "I've never seen anyone do this. It sounds insane. Humm."

EB - "There's no way it could be that simple or easy, so I'm not gonna do that." SE - "Here, I have my brilliant body." UE - "And I have so much practice not listening!" UN - "Why would I start now?" CH - "Wait, maybe I could start listening to the wisdom of my body?"

CB - "No, I don't want to!" UA - "Yes. I do want to receive wisdom from my body." LP - "This is crazy. I'd be crazy to start following guidance from my own body." WR - "But maybe that is the insanity of this world - to not listen to our bodies?" TH - "What I have done in the past is not working for me. I could be available to work with my body and find new outcomes moving forward."

Okay. Wow. Pause for a minute. Sometimes it is actually very valuable to pause. Let the ripples go through you.

Take some deep breaths. Notice what shifted and changed during that round. How are you feeling in your body?

Shame and Anger

I want to shift over to a tapping round for clearing what comes up with the default set up phrase.

I know that it is common to trip on the standard 'I love and accept myself' lingo. Many of us are not congruent there and have difficulty saying, 'I completely love and accept myself.'

When you bring up aspects of money, there are the obviously related things like any experience you've ever had with someone owing you money or trying to collect money from you. Those are personal experiences that impact how you consciously think and feel about your value. You will want to tap on those specific stories.

But there are other layers of emotion that need attention. Implanted ideas about self-worth, praise and appreciation, especially from your earliest experience of someone rewarding or punishing you.

Whether the reward was money or candy or the gift of their presence; when they said, 'you did a good job', or they said, 'you've failed,' 'you can't have the reward.'

How you felt at that time impacted what you made that event mean about yourself. It was printed into the underlying core data of your personality.

That is what we are looking for. Do you have an earlier experience of someone either rewarding you or punishing you?

Participant: By withholding something? Yes, I mean, honestly, from infancy.

Kathy: Can you tell me more about that?

151

Participant: My mother had severe postpartum depression.

Kathy: Okay. Severe depression. Was she hospitalized? Start with that.

Participant: She wasn't there with me. I was with my grandparents. They did love me, but it was different. Yeah.

Kathy: Anytime you're gonna tell a story or pull something up, go ahead and be tapping. That way you can begin to move the energy at the same time you're talking about it.

Also, I invite you all to tap through this process, even if you think these are not your topics. 'Borrowing Benefits' from someone else's tapping journey can be powerful. Okay?

Tapping the side of the hand. Repeat after me, KC - "Even though talking about my coming into the world brought up a lot of emotion ... Right now, I choose to love myself. When I was little, my mom couldn't be with me. I know that and my body feels it still. And today, as who I am now, I lovingly embrace myself. I lovingly embrace all of me, and especially that infant who needed attention and love. I know that I was not held and embraced by my mother, and I love who I am."

EB - "Postpartum depression." SE - "My mother struggled with my birth." UE - "I was a hardship in some ways." UN - "I didn't want to be a hardship for my mother." CH - "But I knew that it was hard for her. I felt it."

152

CB - "Long before I had any words to speak, I felt rejected." UA - "I felt abandoned. I felt that I was lacking worth." LP - "I misunderstood my mother's struggle as something to do with me." WR - " I thought that her not holding me was because she didn't want to hold me." TH - "My mom struggled with depression after my birth. That has been the thing that I know."

EB - "Today I acknowledge that my body struggled too." SE - "My little body didn't understand what happened." UE - "There was no way to communicate my needs and they didn't help me feel safe when my mother was missing." UN - "Right away. I wasn't safe." CH - "I wasn't protected and held."

CB - "I wasn't nurtured by my mother." UA - "I was not held close to my mother, and I've been missing that." LP - "I've been missing nurturing from my mother and feeling ashamed." WR - "Postpartum depression is a real thing for mothers and for babies." TH - " I honor my experience. I was the infant missing the mother. I was completely confused and ashamed."

EB - "Postpartum confusion." SE - "It was my birthday, and I was confused." UE - "It was my birthday, and I was not celebrated." UN - "Postpartum confusion and shame." CH - "Isolation, confusion, withdrawal, shame and lack of celebration."

CB - "It wasn't fair." UA - "It wasn't fair! She had no joy for me." LP - "And I could not find joy for myself either." WR - "Postpartum struggle and shame. This happened to me." TH - "I acknowledge that my body has been holding this content my whole life. Dear body, I'm sorry that you've held this for so long."

EB - "Body thank you for waiting all this time for me to be ready." SE - "I see you now. I appreciate what you've been through." UE - "I give permission for this to be released." UN - "Every bit of all of it. Every bit of residue." CH - "Every memory and feeling of that loss, being held in every cell, I'm willing for it to go now."

CB - "I let it drain out of my organs and meridian pathways and go for recycling to the earth." UA - "I love you baby. Thank you for holding this until I was ready." LP - "I am here with you now and we no longer need to carry this heaviness." WR - "I offer myself now a loving mother's embrace. I now receive these frequencies of kindness and nurturing." TH - "Even though I never had my mother to hold me because postpartum struggle was real for my mother and for me."

EB - "I was the child who struggled with shame." SE - "I am opening space for this postpartum shame to leave my physiology." UE - "I give permission for this release of shame and confusion on every layer of my body and being." UN - "The residue from all of this struggle with shame can go now." CH - "It served its purpose."

CB - "It has shaped my life and I honor that I have been on a lifelong journey with shame." UA - "I lovingly embrace all aspects of myself, and I appreciate myself in ways no one else can." LP - "I offer the mother's embrace for myself, and I choose to receive and feel the nurturing of my mother." Deep breath. WR - "Now and across my timeline." TH - "I receive the energy transfer and allow that integration of nurturing to land in my body here and now."

Just feel for a moment, notice your feet. Notice your legs and your hips and back... All along your spine.

Breathe into your lungs. Maybe roll your shoulders and stretch your arms wide.

Participant: I noticed that this point was really sore on my ribs. (Liver Point.)

Kathy: That can be just lymphatic congestion, but if you're aware of a topic that has anger around it, you might just go to that Liver point on your ribs and tap there as you talk about it. Are you willing to do some tapping rounds about anger?

Participant: Yeah. Yes, definitely.

Kathy: Can you think of your youngest/ earliest experience with anger? A time when you were just livid about something. Or a really strong memory when you thought it meant something about you?

Participant: I know. I got into an argument with my brother. And I … I took a bowl with a big rim, and I smashed it on the kitchen table. I smashed it. There was a chip that flew up and went in my eye. And so, we actually had to go to the hospital. And I think, I mean, I remember that.

I remember being so angry that I did that. And then the consequences of it and then feeling ashamed too. You know that kind of feeling ashamed of myself for reacting so strongly and violently. And, you know, hurting myself. But also, I'm sure it was threatening to my younger brother.

Kathy: Let's start off tapping on the side of the hand. You've already done quite a bit of the negative. We'll just add in, KC - "Even though all of That happened I love who I am. I appreciate that sometimes everybody has big emotions. This thing happened. It wasn't pretty. I'm not proud of it and I love who I am. It is a part of my experience... This fight with my brother and the consequences afterwards."

EB - "So much anger, so much anger." SE - "I was so mad." UE - "Madder than I'd ever been." UN - "Part of me was right!" CH – "I was right to demonstrate my anger."

CB - "He needed to know how mad I was." UA - "How seriously mad I was."

Participant: I think I remember now., You know, it might have been my mom that made me mad.

Kathy: Okay. Next point.

LP - I was mad. My brother was right there. I've been thinking it was about my brother." WR - "Because he was right there." TH - "But my mom was there too. It might have had something to do with my mom."

EB - "There was a lot of anger." SE - "More anger than I could contain." UE - "It just bubbled up through me." UN - "It burned through me." CH - "Some of it escaped from me that day."

CB - "There was violence and breaking, wanting to destroy! Mom was there somewhere." UA - "She wasn't helping me. She hadn't told me or shown me how to *be with* this much anger." LP - "How to deal with this much anger." WR - "It was overwhelming. It was scary. I didn't know what to do with it and I broke a dish." TH - "At the moment, it felt like the best thing I could do. It felt like the best thing to do!"

EB - "The anger was so big!" SE - "I was right there..." UE - "and it took over." UN - "I was out of control." CH - "Overwhelmed and swept away."

CB - "But then there was pain!" UA - "Oh my! There was screaming and yelling and rushing." LP - "And then there was sorrow. There was grief." WR - "No amount of apology could put the bowl back together or repair the damage." TH - "I could see when my parents looked at me. How disappointed they were. How confused, and worried for me. So many big and confusing emotions."

EB - "There was anger." SE - "There was shame." UE - "There is guilt." UN - "There is regret. They all happened so quickly, and I thought it was about my brother." CH - "He was just witnessing while I had this as my experience.

CB - "This is my experience. I thought it meant something about who I am." UA - "But now I have a choice to make about what it will mean to me in the future." LP - "I am willing to wonder, What else could it mean?" WR - "Could it mean anything other than what I was thinking it meant?" TH - "Well, what if I'm human? What if I AM human!?"

EB - "What if these things are the expression of a normal range of emotions?" SE - "What if it was an accident?" UE - "What if it was an accident that I was harmed?" UN - "What if anger is something that happens sometimes?" CH - "What if having anger, and even smashing things, does not have to result in harm?"

CB - "Smashing something doesn't have to result in harm to anyone." UA - "What if I could have my anger and feel safe?" LP - "What if I could help my anger, witness

157

my anger and make room for my anger," WR - "even express my anger and not experience harm?" TH - "Dear body, I'm so sorry that that event of pain came so quickly after the anger."

EB - "I'm sorry for anywhere, those were collapsed as being the same thing." SE - "I'm sorry for everywhere we've been holding ourselves back from the expression of anger for fear of causing sharp physical pain." UE - "Those were clearly confused." UN - "We have believed that anger equals physical pain." CH - "Anger does not equal physical pain."

CB - "Hi body. Anger and pain are not the same thing." UA - "Anger and pain are not the same thing." LP - "Childhood mistakes are not always so intensely painful." WR - "Disappointing my parents is not the same as physical pain." TH - "Emotional pain is not the same as physical pain."

EB - "Physical pain is not the same thing as shame." SE - "Regret and physical pain don't have to go together." UE - "These things do not have to go together." UN - "Dear body, I'm sorry. That was such a confusing event." CH - "That was an intense, painful and confusing event."

CB - "And all the yelling and rushing and panic from my parents made it more complicated." UA - "I responded poorly." LP - "And my parents responded poorly." WR - I admit that I had learned my poor response -ability from those parents." TH - "And then they were mad at me for showing them what they were doing."

Deep breath.

EB - "That didn't make sense to any of us." SE - "We were all confused and panicked and angry." UE - "It didn't make sense to me." UN - "And I've been holding it all this time." CH - "Wow. Thank you, body."

CB - "I love you and I appreciate all you've done for me." UA - "We have so many capacities." LP - "I'm so sorry." WR - "We've been using them to store pain, regret and shame." TH - "I was holding pain, regret and shame in my body. I don't need to carry those now."

Wiggle. Breathe. Stretch. Maybe stand up and walk around a little.

So, come back to the topic of money and check in again. One of the things that has been happening is that while we've been off doing this recent tapping, the other rounds about financial stress and worry have been continuing to integrate through your system.

But because we opened with that topic of money, and then went and asked for these other earlier experiences and memories, they will have been pulling also on the threads that are related to your current money reality.

So now, coming back to today to reassess your SUDS levels. Remember what you remember and just as a reference acknowledge that 'I do have valid reasons to be angry or worried about money.' How do you feel about that sentiment now?

Participant: Honestly, I feel exhausted. Holy moly! It was amazing how much I just … It was like putting down something very heavy. I've been working, this body has been working so hard. Carrying all that stuff, and I really am ready. My body is fine to release it!

159

Kathy: Big changes can show up feeling like a wave of exhaustion. It may take a little while for your body to restabilize into a new pattern.

All that energy that you've been using to hold those old things in place, as your reality, becomes available for creating and generating your future.

That's part of the reason why I say, 'tap on everything you can think of!' It may feel strange, but your life will improve.

When you're in the car, driving with the radio can be a great chance to work short EFT sessions into your schedule. If there's something grabbing your attention on the radio, notice. 'Oh, this song, or commercial reminds me of this (Person /Event /Fear) .' Then just talk and tap through the acupoints. See where it goes.

Another option would be to set and keep a regular appointment with yourself. The easiest one for me is to do tapping for a few minutes any time I'm waiting for the bathtub to fill up.

You could choose to pick a day and sit down to tap alone or with a practitioner. Maybe get a notebook to track your topics and SUDS levels so you can see where you're progressing.

Most people forget what was bothering them when it starts to improve. As the discomfort moves away from their starting SUDS level, they become distracted because they feel so much better than where they were! I hope that you will want to see your SUDS levels getting lower than 3 and even all the way to a 0. Won't that be great? You can actually just be present while enjoying your life!

Releasing Money Madness

We're gonna put our feet flat on the floor. Get comfortable in your chair. Sit up and breathe into lengthening your spine. Relax across your shoulders. Feel your toes and the bottoms of your feet.

Press each foot into the floor and feel how solid the ground is under each foot. Without standing, just press left, then right, left, then right and notice that you could stand up if you wanted to get up. This process helps to orient your body into this moment and realize that you are safe right now.

We're beginning on the karate chop point. Left or right hand. I am also going to invite you to slow down your tapping for these rounds. So instead of using a quick tap, tap, tap, tap, tap try for more of a slow bop, bop, bop application.

With any topic that gets you riled up or agitated like money, you may benefit from actually slowing down your tapping. Okay?

So, we'll have to see if we can keep up the slower pace. Repeat after me, out loud.

KC - "Even though money continues to be a problem, right now, today, I love and accept myself. I love myself right now. I choose to approve of who I am, even though money has not been easy. I don't have financial freedom and today I open the space to love who I am."

Take a deep breath.

EB - "This money agitation." SE - "So much money irritation." UE - "I have all of this roughness around money. I have experienced uncomfortable things." UN - "Some of it is mine. A lot of it is not mine." CH - "All of this financial convolution." Deep breath.

CB - "Money struggles and confusion." UA - "Money agitations." LP - "I've been working so hard. I am working so hard." WR - "I learned a lot of what does not work and I'm tired." TH - "Monetary exhaustion. I'm worn out! I've been through so much." Deep breath.

EB - "I don't like to struggle with money. This fighting is not what I want." SE - "What do I want? I don't like this." UE - "I'm not sure. I'm not sure what needs to change." UN - "I am sure something needs to change." CH - "I know I am here. I have choices to make about my money situation."

CB - "Other people will have their opinions." UA - "Other people will have their emotions." LP - "They may say they know what's best for me." WR - "The truth is, I know what's best for me in my situation." TH - "My situation, my life, my choice. Day to day, moment to moment, it is mine to create." Deep breath.

EB - "I claim, acknowledge, honor and own the reality of my choices." SE - "There have been consequences." UE - "There have been confusions." UN - "There have been problems." CH - "I acknowledge all of these things related to money and my financial choices."

CB - "Right now, I embrace all of who I am, and I offer myself my own trust, patience and kindness." Deep breath. UA - "I am willing to acknowledge what I don't know." LP - "I'm willing to ask for guidance from capable sources." WR - "I am willing to receive instructions," TH - "And I maintain the right to make my own choices based on the information available to me in each circumstance." Take a breath.

Pause for a minute. Stretch.

That was fairly mellow. But what did that bring up? There were some big yawns in there.

Participant: For me it was like, I thought about that this week. There were all these things that made me different. I have so many parts of each experience that may pertain to the problem I'm having now - How do I figure out what needs my time with tapping?

There is a great thing about the record of these EFT scripts. You can go through it again several times. When there is a tangent, you can pause and go tap on that with no worries about missing what the group processed.

Branching off again and again from the same root phrase lets you be very thorough in your personal journey to clarity.

It's your emotional SUDS level that will show you which branches of thought and memory need your time tapping.

If there's an aspect at a level 8 here, a 2, a 4 and a 7 on another aspect, you will probably attend to the 8 first and then the 7 before addressing the 4 and the 2. Just because the items at 8 and 7 were louder and more uncomfortable.

However, that initial aspect at an 8 SUDS level may clear out other aspects as you discharge the electrical component of those memories and emotions.

It can work the other way too.

Weekly or daily tapping to resolve small irritations can ripple those frequencies of peace into your body and teach your system to release big problems long before you address them directly.

You might want to learn about the 'Personal Peace Procedure' by Jessica Ortner.

Let's go back to tapping at the side of the hand.

KC - "Even though my money reality does not yet match, the vision that I have of what is possible, I embrace all of me. I approve of who I am and all that I have been through. There is a discrepancy with my money situation and my financial targets." Deep breath. "Sometimes, I feel that I let myself down and I love myself and I love who I am right now."

EB - "Sometimes I have failed to come up with the money to meet a deadline." SE - "Money seems to be slippery and convoluted." UE - "There are so many layers of emotion connected to money." UN - "I have experienced betrayal and failure and disappointment with money." CH - "Just like people, sometimes I think money is not my friend."

CB - "Sometimes I think money is avoiding me. Or money is mad at me for some reason." Deep breath. UA - "Money is not a person. Money does not hold grudges." LP - "Money does not direct money itself." WR - "Money itself does not physically avoid me." TH - "There is an energy that surrounds money that I can work with or choose to avoid. My opinions about money inform each situation."

EB - "When I feel unworthy. When I feel guilty or ashamed, I project that money should not come to me." SE - "Money is money." UE - "I broadcast how I feel, and money simply follows those instructions." UN - "Money is money." CH - "I sometimes radiate the fear that money will go somewhere else... So, it does."

CB - "Money is money. I am me. I have my money reality fixed in my mind." UA - "Reality is mine to choose, and it is my mind to change." LP - Sometimes. I will tell such an amazing story about how money has betrayed me. It left me high and dry!" WR - "I make money out to be the bad guy and a villain in my life." TH - "When money is just money."

EB - "Having my story lets me be entertained." SE - "and my stories help me commiserate with other people who personify money that way too." UE - "But money itself is just money." UN - "There are lots of energies and frequencies around money." CH - "I might say 'I want money to love me.' and wait for the chance to feel that somehow."

CB - "I want money to be with me for the long term." UA - "I want money to want me the way I want money." LP - "I've made a money personality of lack and longing as though it's romantic." WR - "I've made money as a psychotic, tumultuous or petty lover." TH - "I've made my money show up as an angry parent who punishes me with long absences."

EB - "I've collapsed and confused my emotional childhood with my financial reality now." SE - "My emotional confusion becomes my financial confusion." UE - "My childhood misunderstanding of love clouds my experience of financial freedom." UN - "What is love? What is money?" CH - "Is there a difference?" Deep breath.

CB - "What is approval? Is it having money?" UA - "What is money? Is giving money giving love?" LP - "I want there to be a difference. Is there a difference?" WR - "As a child I could not tell the difference." TH - "I was so confused. Maybe my parents didn't know that they were confusing me."

EB - "The odds are high that they were confused about money too." SE – "I can see from their behaviors that they were confused," UE - "And that they did not know the difference." UN - "Is there a difference between physical money and money as an energy?" CH - "What is the difference between tangible money, the energy of money and the illusion of money?"

CB - "There are the illusions of money too!" UA - "Illusions of love personified and the bastardization of worth." LP - "Bastardization, like a fairy godmother that will come and solve all our financial problems." WR - "Money is not a fairy godmother, and no amount of money will ever be a genie in a bottle either." TH - "No amount of money, cash-in-hand or in my bank account will ever be a real wishing well!" Deep breath

EB - "Childhood fascination, distortion and confusion." SE - "I wanted to understand money and love." UE - "The people teaching me did not understand and could not teach me." UN - "Wow. Right now. I realize that I have collapsed the personification of money with the energy of money and love." CH - "Right now, I recognize that they are not the same thing." Take a deep breath.

CB - "The fairytales of money, love, and relationships... It is just a story." UA - "For me to have healthy forms of money in my life," LP - "or to have healthy love in relationships..." WR - "I need to show up and not wait to be saved." TH - "I can't wait for money to choose me first, or for someone else to approve of me, value and desire me."

EB - "There are things I get to do." SE - "There are actions that I will take." UE - "There are questions that I can ask." UN - "If I'm waiting for magic to happen, I get to keep waiting." CH - "If I'm waiting for some external personification of money to change my life for me, I will never have my financial outcomes land in my physical reality."

CB - "If I persist in waiting for a financial fantasy, I will never have my financial outcomes." Deep breath. UA - "Money is money." LP - "I can have money and choose money." WR - "I can spend money, I can keep money." TH - "I can donate money. I can lose money. I can make more money."

EB - "Money is an object. It has value when I give it value." SE - "I have value with or without money." UE - "Money has value as a tradeable currency even when I project all of my childhood confusion onto it." UN - "I have permission to feel whatever I would like to feel about money." CH - "I see money for what it is and for what it is not."

CB - "I see money as a currency and I pull my old fantasies away." UA - "Everywhere I invested in an emotional projection about the fantasies of money, I call that energy back to me now for recycling." LP - "I choose to unravel, unbind, and dissipate the fantasies of my mind." WR - "Financial fantasies have been a distraction and I release them now." TH - "Money is money. Just waiting for me to create my reality. There it is. Money is waiting for me to say how it can come to me. And what we will do together."

EB - "I have choices to make about my financial reality." SE - "I see that when I am joyful; when I am happy and content that I open the door and invite money to find me." UE - "When I am sorrowful; when I am angry, then I close the door and I tell the energy of money to stay away." UN - "When I breathe and find my feet and I show up things are different." CH - "I have the choice to acknowledge my awareness and to be present with each aspect of here and now." Take a deep breath. Long slow inhalation. Longer, slower exhalation.

CB - "From that place of awareness I am an invitation." UA - "I can follow where the current of currency is flowing." LP - "I let my body show me where there is more joyful creation." WR - "And in building my happiness I can be even more of an invitation for receiving." TH – "Money is money. It has many forms and many ways to land in my open hands." Deep breath.

EB - "Money is money." SE - "I am who I am, and I am open to new possibilities with money." UE - "Space opens around me and in my bank accounts for receiving joyful currencies." UN - "I invite healthy and vibrant interactions with money." CH - "I know that pragmatic, calm, sustainable…"

CB - "reasonable, accessible…" UA - "beautiful, harmonious… " LP - "expansive, luxurious…" WR -

"comforting, graceful…" TH - "lucrative, generative, generous, miraculous and mundane sources of income are available to me now."

Check in. Take a few deep breaths. Go ahead and stretch. That was an extensive session. Take some time to be with all of those ripples moving through your body and mind.

I Feel Like a Fraud

I want to share something with you. It's from a very well-known American financial advisor.

She said, "It wasn't until I stood in my truth and told everybody that I had $250,000 in credit card debt. At that point, everything turned around for me. I had to reveal the truth about what I didn't have, more than pretend about what I did. That was interesting." - Suze Orman

Consider that for a minute.

How much discrepancy is happening in your own financial life? Is there a difference between the way you feel on the inside with your money versus how you want the world to see you?

Is there a little gap, or a big one?

Make a note for yourself about the starting SUDS level around the energy of feeling like a fraud with your money and financial success.

Let's begin. For this section I'm going to have you tap through clearing statements adapted from the tools of Access Consciousness™ to release the stuck energy of entities connected to this topic of fraudulent or hollow success.

Either rub the sore spot under your collarbone or use the side of the hand and tap.

KC - "Even though I'm so tired and I feel like a fraud, right now I embrace who I am. I give myself approval even though I'm exhausted and this money stuff is hard work. I don't feel up to the task of matching who I am with who I'd like to be and even with all of that going on I love who I am."

EB - "All that [that] is, known and unknown." SE - "Agreements, oaths, bindings…" UE - "contracts, commitments or curses…" UN - "with me, for me, about me" CH - "or anyone else regarding money,"

CB - "from this or any timeline; I destroy and uncreate it now." UA - "I revoke, recant, rescind, renounce and denounce all that that is or was." LP - "Any entities hired for the purpose of maintaining struggle with money," WR - "or keeping me bound to feeling like a fraud," TH - "your services here are no longer desired or required."

EB – "You all have to go now." SE - "Take with you all of your chemical and magnetic," UE - "imprinting, binding and bonding." UN - "Return to from whence you came." CH - "Never to return to me, my body,"

CB - "this planet or this reality. Across all time space dimensions and realities. Thank you." UA - "I give thanks to all aspects of me," LP - "and to all energies who participated in any way," WR - "to clear these frequencies completely." TH - "Out of my system and out of my field." Take a deep breath. Feel what is shifting.

I recommend using the Access entity clearings anytime you have a harsh or nagging voice in your head telling you that you can't, or you shouldn't do something.

If you are thinking something like 'Why try? I'll just mess it up.' Challenge that thought! Learn to interrupt with 'Wait, who are you? Get out!'

The same way you would not entertain the company of a physical person criticizing and demeaning you in your home; the entities do not have a right to trash your headspace and tear at your emotion's day and night."

Entities can latch onto us like a hitchhiker or leech in our aura. They will stay until you make declarations like 'You have no business here. I live here now. You have to go and take your crap with you!'

So how are you feeling? Lighter is the hope.

Clearing entities can help open up space for more ease with all types of creation. Particularly if you were carrying an entity, or group addicted to drama or substances - having them leave can be life changing.

Let's do more tapping for releasing fraud and that energy of not feeling up to the task of life.

KC - "Even though I often don't know what I'm doing, I love that about me. Right now, I give my full approval for Every bit of myself just because I can. Especially when I feel like a fraud; like a fake and any minute they're gonna come get me, I choose to love me. I'm so proud of myself! I've done so much, even when I felt like a fraud."

EB - "Yep, I'm a fraud." SE - "There's a whole lot I don't know." UE - "In fact, I know just enough to know there's a lot I don't know!" UN - "I shouldn't be doing the things I'm doing." CH - "There's probably a million people more qualified than I am."

CB - "It might be only a thousand. But I actually prefer for there to be somebody more qualified." UA - "I want somebody else to take over!" LP - "I was starting to get good at being a kid and then I had to be a grown up." WR - "It kind of just snuck up on me." TH - "I wasn't done being a kid and then I was in charge!? That's a real bummer."

EB - "Here I am, feeling like a fraud." SE - "Is feeling like a fraud and a fake actually a way to feel safe? Wow." UE - "If I feel like a fraud, I won't get cocky and arrogant." UN - "Maybe feeling like a fraud helps me look humble." CH - "Somebody told me that being humble was the best way to be." Take a deep breath.

CB - "Arrogant and confident are not the best way to be." UA - "It's better to be a fraud. It's better to be a fake." LP - "So that if I'm ever challenged, I can just say 'Tada!'" WR - "I DON'T know what I am doing!" TH - "And then they can say, 'Wow, you've done so well for so long.'"

EB - "Versus, if I say I'm an expert," SE - "and I have all the training…" UE - "If I let them think I know what I'm doing," UN - "Or that I'm the best in my field.." CH - "and then I mess up?! That'd be horrible,"

CB - "I can't imagine! Except I do imagine being in that mess." UA - "If I am at the top of the heap there is nowhere to hide." LP - "I don't want to be the one responsible." WR - "I don't want to have that authority." TH - "I want somebody else to be in charge." Deep breath.

EB - "No. I don't want that either." SE - "I resent the people that try to control me. Try to be in charge of me." UE - "I dare you to take charge of me." UN - "But I don't want to be in charge of everything either." CH - "I don't want to be wrong. I don't want to be a fraud or be a fake."

CB - "I don't want to be a fraud. I don't want I don't want to be fake." UA - "If I have this sensitivity to feeling like a fraud and fake." LP - "Maybe that will keep me authentic?" WR - "Authentic? I would prefer to have authenticity." TH - " I'm hyper vigilant for anywhere I might be fraudulent or look fraudulent."

EB - "What if that's in the way of my authenticity?" SE - "I'm so carefully avoiding being fraudulent. I can't have my authenticity." UE - "Avoiding fraud, I am also avoiding confidence." UN - "Hyper vigilance about being a fraud and a fake." CH - "This energy keeps me very close to being a fraud."

CB - "This behavior keeps that problem active in my field. It keeps it alive so that people wonder about me." UA – "It's really normal. Most people feel that way." LP - "Most people feel that they weren't done being a child," WR - "when they had to start being a grown up." TH - "So in some ways, almost everyone feels like a fraud."

EB - "Everyone feels overwhelmed sometimes." SE - "I've been feeling like a fraud but I'm not alone." UE - "It's a very common thing and I love that about me." UN - "I love that about me." CH - "I have this in common with most people, but I felt alone."

CB - "Sometimes I do know what I'm doing." UA - "I know I don't want fraud and I don't want fakeness." LP - "I can choose to be honest and authentic." WR - "I can practice vulnerability and presence with myself and in my relationships." TH - I open space for authenticity. I open space for confidence and self-respect in my life."

EB - "Since I'm not going to let anybody else be in charge, I could do it." SE - "I could choose to take charge of my life." UE - "And when I'm choosing to choose, I get to rearrange things." UN - "I get to decide what it is to be authentic." CH - "I get to decide what is my best and when I have done enough."

CB - "Right now I honor, acknowledge and approve of myself." UA - "I know that I do my best to honorably navigate each day." LP - "My standard within myself has been so high." WR - "I push myself beyond what anyone else would ever ask of me." TH - "I choose now to honor, acknowledge and accept the evidence that who I am is good enough." Deep breath.

EB - "I am authentic and sincere." SE - "I am powerful and capable." UE - "My sincerity is enough." Deep breath. UN - "I honor and respect my efforts each day." CH - " I acknowledge my sincerity and my progress."

CB - "I fully embrace who I have been, and I choose to move forward now." UA - "I bring honesty, curiosity and presence with me as my companions." LP - "This is new for me to claim my strengths." WR - "I choose to travel through life with self-respect and authenticity as my companions too." TH - "Together we can do so much! I open the space for finding out what kind of Mastery I can achieve."

Stretch. You may need to stand up or go for a walk after that series.

Wiggle, wiggle, wiggle. The electrical components in your brain are probably firing extra mapping and rippling through different connections. Keep wiggling and moving gently because we are asking the filing system in our brain to take labels off of folders, rearrange content and reassign things; to delete this and throw that out, and tie this to make a new association over here.

Be gentle with your mind and body for the next little while.

Do you need more water, more sugar or more salt? Do what works for your body.

The Invitation of Gratitude

Participant: Would it help us to listen to this content at night? I mean like, as quiet background noise. To play it even if we're sleeping. Or do you actually have to be tapping along with the program?

Kathy: I reserve nighttime tracks for content I definitely want embedded into my psyche. Recording your own voice with affirmations might be more powerful than this mixture of group work and discussions. That's up to you though.

For the question about active versus passive participation. When you're new to the process of tapping, they do recommend that you do the tapping physically on your acupoints while speaking out loud.

Then later, as you get more accustomed to tapping and acquainted with it, your body knows what tapping is. There is a point, a threshold, where you can shift a lot of content for yourself by just thinking through, or remembering what it is like to stimulate the acupoints in your head.

And then yes, beyond that you can think about your topic, and you can think about tapping and experience shifting in your meridian pathways.

Touch is still a good thing. I recommend tapping the points if you are somewhere you feel comfortable using EFT. You are also learning about having safe, therapeutic touch when you are using meridian tapping accurately.

You do always have your finger points that are easy to do under the table. Those acupoints are located by the base of the nail on the top of each finger.

If you point your thumb to the sky, and then hit every finger with your thumb on the way down - those are your acupoints for tapping. You can use your thumb on either hand to touch the side of each finger of the same hand.

Also, when people are drumming their fingers on the table, they're actually stimulating acupressure points and helping to reset their system whether they know it or not.

Participant: Sometimes after a session I'm not sure about my SUDS level. It's like I need a minute for the wave of energy shifting to slosh through me. I think I need to integrate and pause a little before I can have an assessment of what just happened.

Kathy: Good job noticing! That is very accurate. We do often need time for integration and recalibration after several rounds of tapping, on any subject. That period of integration can be about 5 minutes and other times several hours.

Ready for another layer?

There is a book called "Power vs Force" by David R Hawkins. He created a map of consciousness (Image B) that shows the spectrum of thoughts and emotion, having lower vibrations associated with force and higher vibrations aligned with power. He demonstrates how we can with consciousness, intention, and discernment, find truth and follow it toward a more fulfilled and impactful life.

Map of Consciousness

MAP OF CONSCIOUSNESS

STRONG ← | → WEAK

POWER ← | → FORCE

God-view	Life-view	Level	Scale	Emotion	Process
Self	Is	Enlightenment	700-1000	Ineffable	Pure Consciousness
All-Being	Perfect	Peace	600	Bliss	Illumination
One	Complete	Joy	540	Serenity	Transfiguration
Loving	Benign	Love	500	Reverence	Revelation
Wise	Meaningful	Reason	400	Understanding	Abstraction
Merciful	Harmonious	Acceptance	350	Forgiveness	Transcendence
Inspiring	Hopeful	Willingness	310	Optimism	Intention
Enabling	Satisfactory	Neutrality	250	Trust	Release
Permitting	Feasible	Courage	200	Affirmation	Empowerment
Indifferent	Demanding	Pride	175	Scorn	Inflation
Vengeful	Antagonistic	Anger	150	Hate	Aggression
Denying	Disappointing	Desire	125	Craving	Enslavement
Punitive	Frightening	Fear	100	Anxiety	Withdrawal
Disdainful	Tragic	Grief	75	Regret	Despondency
Condemning	Hopeless	Apathy	50	Despair	Abdication
Vindictive	Evil	Guilt	30	Blame	Destruction
Despising	Miserable	Shame	20	Humiliation	Elimination

The Emotional Guidance Scale

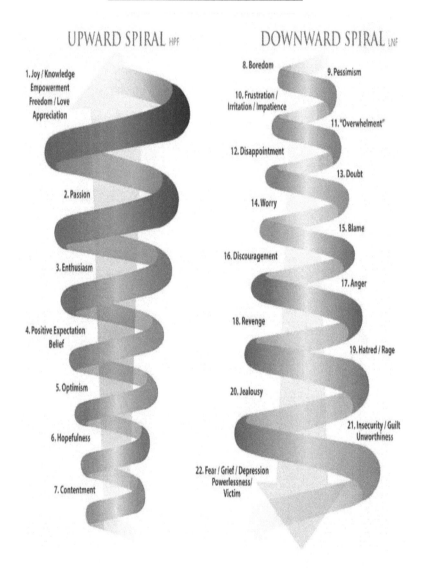

With these images in mind, check in with yourself about the idea of 'I am an invitation for money to come play with me."

What comes up? How big is the feeling? Make notes, and let's tap for that.

Rub the sore spot or begin tapping at the side of the hand. KC - "Even though I don't feel like there are enough ways for money to get to me I love me. Right now, today, or just for the next few minutes … I choose to celebrate who I am. Even though I don't participate with having money. There's too much going on with money. And it's all too complicated, I love who I am."

EB - "Money, money, money, money, money." SE - "Money and debt." UE - "Past expenditures and bills." UN - "Credit card balances and due dates." CH - "Stress and interest charges."

CB - "Money coming in. Money going out." UA - "Money concerns." LP - "Financial confusions." WR - "Financial convulsions." TH - "There is always something about money."

EB - "Anybody you talk to could tell you something bad or painful about money." SE - "Nobody wants to hear from someone who's having total ease and joy." UE - "That's not a popular thing. Having ease with money." UN - "It ought to be normal." CH - "We could celebrate people who are doing well. But it's easier to be frustrated."

CB - "It's easier to be jealous and angry." UA - "It's easier to be confused. Why do they get to have ease and joy?" LP - "When I have frustration and struggle with money." WR - "All this time spent expressing anger,

181

frustration, jealousy and confusion." TH - "I've been broadcasting on the topic of money! Radiating anger, frustration, jealousy, and fear … As though that's normal."

EB - "What if money was out there, as a being or intelligence," SE - " listening and waiting for the right time to show up in my life?" UE - "I've been blaring bad news, regret and shame." UN - "If I were money, I think I'd run the other way." CH - "I have not been inviting money with my thoughts, emotions or actions."

CB - "It's not my fault. I know it's what I have learned." UA - "It's what I have experienced from other people. And right now, I know that doesn't work for them." LP - "I know it doesn't work for me." WR - "I know I can't jump from financial misery, struggle and money madness to joy with money." TH - "I can start to notice when those things come up. They are old habits. They lower my vibrations, drive money away and close down my awareness." Take a deep breath.

EB - "When I notice old things running in me, I can choose to raise my frequencies." SE - "I can change the music, physically in my environment." UE - "I can change the frequency of my emotions and my thoughts." UN - "I can change my thoughts. I can change my actions." CH - "First I notice. I witness and evaluate. What's going on here?"

CB - "Does this behavior work for me?" UA - "Who does this belong to?" LP - "Is this pattern of thinking and behavior even mine? Probably not." WR - "Would I like to do something different? What would it take to change my outcomes?" TH - "What energies and emotions would I like to have in my life?"

EB - "Hope and acceptance feel better than worry." SE - "I can find lots of things to hope for." UE - "A moment of hope and acceptance, for a person or for an animal could help." UN - "I could let an animal change my mood." CH - "I can spend time appreciating and being grateful for an animal or a child."

CB - "When I change my focus, I change my thinking." UA - "I change my thinking and my mood shifts." LP - "When I change my mood, I can have a different experience." WR - "I'm not going to jump from money madness to joyful adventure all at once." TH - "But I can choose to move in that direction. I can make new pathways in my brain."

EB - "I can choose new habits and new patterns." SE - "I can release money madness." UE - "I choose to witness the old patterns of disharmony." UN - "I choose to acknowledge what is not working for me." CH - "And whenever I notice I give permission for things to change."

CB - "In the witnessing I can find joy. It could be a tiny bit funny." UA - "When I see that I'm running an old pattern I could take a deep breath and say 'Look! Isn't that amazing?' I learned that pattern so well."

LP - "Look at me, being so loyal and showing dedication to my family." WR - "I see these patterns and frequencies running in my life and I smile. I know now that I have other possibilities." TH - "I choose in my witnessing to breathe, soften, and choose again. I am authentic after all."

EB - "Now I am powerful where I was being forceful." SE - "I am resourceful and patient." UE - "I am grateful for my journey and my growth." UN - "I have a lot that I appreciate and more that I love." CH - "I even love and appreciate myself more than I used to."

CB - "I choose to appreciate and grow in gratitude." UA - "And as I am grateful, I begin to be joyful." LP - "I can think about money and gracefully invite money to join me." WR - "Yes. To join me in my life; to join me in my exploration." TH - "Each time I pause to acknowledge old patterns and raise my frequencies I release the inheritance of money madness."

EB - "Each time I open more space. SE - "I invite money to join me in this new space." UE - "I receive money with ease, joy and glory." UN - "I receive myself and money with patience and pleasure." CH - "Other people don't have to join me."

CB - "They don't even have to know that money is getting along with me, and I am getting along with money so well." UA - "It's okay to breathe just for myself. I eat for the benefit of my body." LP - "I could have my relationship and my reality with my money." WR - "I invite Money. I'd like money to be my companion." TH - "I trust myself and I extend that trust to my new relationship with money." Deep breath. "I am authentic. I know that I am powerful. And my money is mine because I am my friend."

EB - "I relax into receiving and other people do Monday madness." SE - "I breathe into my roots even if other people panic." UE - "I let go of fear and expand my heart." UN - "I embrace growth as other people choose hoarding." CH - "I trust and hope where other people have worry and fear." Deep breath.

CB - "I trust myself. And from that trust I know that money is consistently what it is." UA - "I know that it is there for my use, and I trust money to be just as it is." LP - "I don't ask it to be anything it's not." WR - "I am grateful to have my needs met through people who can give me those things that I require." TH - "Money is money. I am resourceful, confident, potent, and authentic." Deep breath.

Little by little we work through the complexity of changing realities and accessing emotional freedom to gain financial freedom.

Little by little we choose to work with patience and kindness to gently extricate ourselves from the dysfunction of our past and create new frameworks for generative and graceful outcomes.

Okay? Yes. Do you need water, sugar, or salt? Anytime you do this work you really are overhauling your system. You are changing your reality! Give yourself a minute to land, and your body a few minutes to integrate.

Some of those aspects we opened will need you to continue tapping. There are likely to be some little bits of related content that float up to the surface. And although you *can* shove them down again, I do not recommend that.

We just did all that work to move things out of the way and allow the deeper layers to surface. So yes, plan for continuing to tap throughout the day whenever another emotion or memory comes up.

It's so much easier to just attend to them in the moment, whether you have words or not. Let it move through and be seen so that you can release the significance and move on.

It is a big thing to change the trajectory of your life. Please take some time to witness and acknowledge the changes that you have made.

Maybe ask a friend to help you reflect on how you used to be, before all this tapping stuff got into your habits.

You will find that your tenacity is good for you.

Money and Relationships

Let's do a generic round first.

This is useful for whatever's going on. Nice and slow because we've been agitated. Tap, Tap, Tap and repeat after me.

KC - "Even though there's so much going on I choose to lovingly embrace myself with grace right now. I'm overwhelmed, overtaxed, and overburdened and I embrace all of who I am. I embrace myself especially because there's so much going on. I give myself my full approval because there's a lot happening and it's happening so fast. I love that about me. I receive and see myself, especially when no one else is seeming to see the gift of who I am."

EB - "A lot of change very quickly." SE - "There's so much change." UE - "So much intensity." UN - "My body is weary." CH - "There's a lot happening right now."

CB - "I have deadlines to meet. There are people pushing me. There are people rushing me." UA - "I have to keep up. I have to jump." LP - "I have to leap. Even if part of me does not want to leap." WR - "And right now change is happening anyway." TH - So much happening. More than I like to deal with. More change than I like to have happening."

EB - "I'm sure there are things happening that I don't know about." SE - "I'm sure there are things I haven't thought of." UE - "Even though my brain is working overtime to keep up." UN - "Even though my body is stressed." CH - "I have to move anyway. I have to go now!"

CB - "I'd like to have time. I'd like to have more choices." UA - "But right now the best I can do is to move quickly." LP - "I don't like to have to move quickly." WR - "But it's what's needed right now." TH - "I have to act. Since I need to participate with what's happening, I choose to choose."

EB - "I open space for the possibility that I can move quickly and accurately." SE - "I open space for knowing that I am capable of dynamic change with speed and grace." UE - "I am willing to find out that I can have accuracy with speed." UN - "This is uncomfortable." CH - "I don't know that it will ever quit being uncomfortable."

CB - "But right now I can open space." UA - "And I give full permission for graceful changes." LP - "I am willing to find out how agile and quick and competent I can be." WR - "I can take breaths and then check in with myself again." TH - "I choose to be adaptable and graceful with speed and accuracy."

Now let's go to the outside of the hand, because we are adding in the financial component. And yes, pause again and check in with what has come up.

How big is your current stress about financial urgency?

KC - "Even though money is complicated already. Sometimes we do money and relationships. Sometimes it's an intimate relationship that involves money. Sometimes it's a business partnership, a landlord or a doctor-patient relationship. I love who I am, and I witness that there are all of these complex financial relationships. There are these relationships that have money as a part of them and I embrace myself and I approve of who I am. Sometimes it's easy. Sometimes it's screwy. Sometimes it's scary and I honor all of my experiences. I have witnessed all of these things. So even though sometimes it's screwy or scary, I love and accept myself."

EB - "Relationships are often complicated." SE - "Money is often complicated." UE - "What was I thinking? How did I get into this situationship?" UN - "I chose to jump in on a relationship and mix it with finances." CH - "I chose to trust and believe that they would have my values and standards." UN - "I thought someone else would have my same ethics and integrity." CH - "Money is complicated."

CB - "My relationships have been complicated." UA - "I've been putting them together. Shaking it up and then wondering what happened!" Deep breath. LP - "But I know I'm never actually in a relationship with myself when I'm dealing with someone else." WR - "I like to project that who I am, in my sincerity, would be who they are." TH - "I have my values. I like to hope that they have my values too! Damn it!! Fuck! It turns out they don't have my honesty and ethical standards."

EB - "I've been swindled! Sadly, I trusted the wrong people." SE - "I lost my money." UE - "I lost my money!" UN - "It was confusing. It was a mess!" CH - "It turns my stomach. I trusted them with so many things!"

CB - "I was in love, and I was an easy mark. I know that now." UA – "I'm a bit jaded and feeling dizzy." LP - "I hate that. I don't want to be jaded." WR - "I don't want to be caught off guard this way." TH - "I want to trust people. But I still want people to have my values and standards!"

EB - "They should not have attacked my sanity and safety!" SE - "I still want other people... specific people to have the integrity that I have." UE - "But obviously I'm not actually in charge of what they do." UN - "And hoping and wishing won't make them be authentic or honest." CH - "I have choices to make about what I do next."

CB - "It is up to me whether or not I trust other people," UA - "whether I trust myself." LP - "I'm not in charge of how they behave." WR - "I can't make them be sincere or authentic." TH - "I am in charge of how I behave and what I think." Deep breath.

EB - "I can get things in writing." SE - "I can make sure there are witnesses." UE - "I can document and clarify what's happening with my money." UN - "I can ask questions." CH - "I can ask questions about my questions and ask for guidance."

CB - "It's okay to be cautious." UA - "I am the one here with me now." LP - "I choose to comfort myself. I choose to breathe." WR - "I am here. I do have integrity with my body." TH - "I will honor my intuition. Even when I love someone, I am willing to know that I know if they are lying to me."

EB - "I open space for my body to tell me clearly." SE - "I am willing for my body to show me and teach me about truth and lies." UE - "I am willing to know when someone makes my body uncomfortable." UN - "Whether it's a professional relationship," CH - "or an emotional relationship."

CB - "Even if there is no money exchanged, I am willing for my body to show me." UA - "Who do you trust? Who do I trust?" LP - "Why do you trust them?" WR -

"Well sometimes my body trusts someone that should not be trusted." TH - "Sometimes I do trust too easily and too quickly."

EB - "But between the two of us, with open dialogue and internal trust; we're more likely to do a better job." SE - "If my body automatically trusts someone, I'm not sure I will ask more questions!" UE - "Who do they remind me of?" UN - "How old am I feeling right now?" CH - "Who am I being right now?"

CB - "If I automatically trust someone because of how they dress but my body is uncomfortable..." UA - "I choose to honor and acknowledge what's going on with my body and get curious." LP - "I commit to being present with my body." WR - "I am willing to ask more questions and resolve whatever conflict arises so that we can be clearer and more integrated." TH - "No matter who's around and no matter what they say."

EB - "Even if they're promising money." SE - "Even if they're promising affection." UE - "Especially if they say that they love me," UN - "I choose to have clarity with my emotions." CH - "I have been flustered and rushed in the past."

CB - "I do not need to rush with love or money." UA - "Moving forward, I choose to move at my own pace with love and with money." LP - "Someone who loves me will give me time to get clear about my financial choices." WR - "I love myself and I respect my time and resources." TH - "I will move forward now with pragmatic and unflustered confidence in myself."

Okay, what came up? What would you like to continue tapping for?

191

Urgency, Bitterness & Sweetness

Participant: We didn't really get to the piece for me specifically about urgency.

Kathy: We can do that. We're going to do our best to tap slowly, even though we're talking about anxiety inducing content.

Actually, let's move to a variation of tapping called 'Touch and Breathe.' You're just going to contact the acupoint and do your best to breathe long and slow at each point.

Any topic that is especially invigorating or upsetting for you, 'Touch and breathe' is a great option to balance and calm down.

Side of the hand. Touch the KC - "Even though there are things that are urgent right now... In these 10 seconds I approve of myself. I choose to love myself, bigger and better than anyone has today. Because I know that I am being rushed and I appreciate the hardship that is on my body, better than anyone else. I love and accept myself. I know what my body requires and right now I offer myself comfort." Breathe.

Just contacting and breathing. EB - "Urgency." SE - "They.... want it done right... now." Breathe. UE - "They want it done right now." UN - "They want it done yesterday." Breathe. Touch the CH - "Hurry... hurry.... "Take a slow breath. "Hurry..."

Touch and breathe. CB - "There is only.... so much time.... each day." Breathe. UA - "There is only ... one of me." Breathe. LP - "But... I have to hurry?" Breathe. WR - "I have to get... it... done." Touch and breathe. TH - "I have to..." Breathe. "The deadline ... is coming.... There isn't any... room past ...the deadline."

EB - Touch and breathe. "It really is a hard... cut off." SE - breath. "I hate deadlines..." Touch and breathe. UE - "I knew it was ..." Touch and breathe. UN - "coming." Breathe. CH - "I thought I was getting ready...."

Touch and breathe. CB - "and I thought I was getting there... on time... "UA - "I'm in the..." Breathe. Touch and breathe. LP - "crunch... time..." Breathe. WR - "and there's no ...." TH - "avoiding it..."

Touch and breathe. EB - "Hurry ...get it done." Touch and breathe. SE - "I don't want.... to." UE - "I have to..." Touch and breathe. UN - "have to..." yawn... CH - "I can... Yes, I can. ..."

Touch and breathe. CB - "I ...won't. I ...won't." Touch and breathe. UA - "I will. I .... will." Touch and breathe. LP - "You... can't ..." Breathe. "Make me..." WR - "... Maybe." Deep breath. "You ... don't have ....to make ...me." Touch and breathe... TH - "I'm making ... myself "breathe. "And I'm ... driving myself."

Touch and breathe. EB - "I mean... I'm." SE - "the one..." Touch and breathe. UE - "I won't even... "Deep breath. "Let me have..." UN - "... a bathroom ... break." Touch and breathe. CH - "Even ... the bathroom."

CB - Touch and breathe. "I want ...ed food... ...Wait. "Deep breath. "Wait..., there is ... no time for... food?" Touch and breathe. UA "...Yes, there is. ".... it's a ... deadline." Breathe "And it's... coming ... fast." UA - Touch and breathe "I do.... feel ...like I'm... alone. And... that..." LP - "it might... be true... It might be." WR - "it might be... a very... harsh cut off." Touch and breathe TH - "There might be.... drastic... consequences..." Breathe.

Touch and breathe EB - "I might ... actually... have to do.... this ...on my own." Touch and breathe SE - "There might... be someone .... who would ... help me..." UE - Touch and breathe. "But I don't ... want to ...find out." UN - "I ... know best." CH - Touch and breathe. "This... it is... is my mess.... I worked ..." Breathe. "Really hard to.... create.... it this way."

Keep going. I know it's hard to slow down this much and to do so much breathing!

CB - Touch and breathe "I'm so... proud of me.... No, I'm.... not." SE - Touch and breathe. "I'm so... embarrassed." Touch and breathe. UE - "Here.... it is right ...at the end.... Here it is. "UN - Breathe "And there.... should not be... this ...much left to do..." CH - Touch and breathe. "Should not be...How it is."

CB - Breathe. Still just touching the points. "I don't want .... anyone to know.... how much ... there is... still to do." UA - "I don't .... want anybody to .... know." LP - "I'm ... too embarrassed.... I'm embarrassed." Touch and breathe. WR - "I'm... alone... and proud." TH - "I'm too... proud to ... "Deep breath. "I'm not gonna ... say anything."

Touch and breathe. EB - "I could... ask for help." SE - "And... they'll say no." Touch and breathe UE - "I... could ask.... for help.... And they might... say yes." UN - Breathe. "They... might say yes." CH - Touch and breathe. "I'm going to.... do it all by myself.... I'm ... going to ...do it all ... I've decided."

194

CB - Touch and breathe. "The only valuable way… is if I …. demonstrate my…. superhuman powers." UA - Touch and breathe. "There are some…. people…. Some people who …. would be …. pissed if they…. find… out next week …." LP - Touch and breathe. "That I …. didn't ask…. them… for help." WR - Touch and breathe. "There are…. people …that… love me. There …are people …that…" TH - Deep breath. "Would love to …show up for me…. I'm … not gonna give …. them the opportunity. I'm the helper… it's…. my job to…. help other people."

Touch and breathe. EB - "I like having…. people indebted to me…. I like having…. to give." SE - Breathe. "I will not …. give them…. an opportunity…. to… reciprocate." UE - Touch and breathe. "Other people…. receive …. help from ….me." Touch and Breath UN - "I'm … a great … helper…. I will not…" CH - Touch and breathe. "I … will not… let …. anyone…. help .. me."

CB - Touch and breathe "I would … just be disappointed…. After … all… I am the best." Touch and breathe - UA - "the best…. no one could …. possibly …do the job…. that I do." LP - Touch and breathe. "So, this is…. mine… I'm gonna…. push myself." WR - Touch and breathe. "I'm gonna … drag it … out…. right up to the last minute." Th - Touch and breathe. "I'll be… exhausted…. or not…. I… don't have…. to do it…… that way…. Maybe I'm…. being unreasonable." Pause. Breathe.

Shift back to regular tapping on the points, but still keep it slow.

EB - "It is mine... I created it this way." SE - "Since I created it, maybe I do have a choice." UE - "And if I'm done having it be the way it is. I could entertain a different

195

possibility." Deep breath. UN - "What if someone would help me?" CH - "What if I could be helped with this project."

CB - "Assistance might be really expensive. It might be free... They might want to hug." UA - "Maybe they would help me and then say, 'Thank you.' Wow. That would be so weird." LP - "And I definitely could not deal with that." WR - "People having gratitude for me. Gratitude for me, from people assisting me?" TH - "I am the helper! I help others. I am so attached to this title. I have worked hard to be the helper... the best helper!" Deep breath.

EB - "It's been fun." SE - "It's been heavy." UE - "No, it hasn't! It has sucked being the best out there." UN - "I've had to demonstrate that 'above and beyond' over and over again." CH - "For thankless people I've worked so hard... with little and no compensation." Deep breath.

CB - "So many times I've been forgotten." SE - "What recognition?" UA - "What compensation?" LP - "But maybe no one ever saw me there." WR - "I have worked quietly and efficiently behind the scenes whenever possible." TH - "Maybe there are people that have seen me... that know who I am and will gladly assist me." Deep breath.

EB - "But I can't ask. But I can't. I can't" SE - "I won't ask." UE - "I won't even ask my team." UN - "My team of non-physical guides and helpers who watch me all day every day." CH - "They're not even allowed to help me! I am demonstrating my superhuman capacities!" Take another deep breath.

CB - "I'm gonna do this all on my own." UA - "You can't stop me." LP - "But I could pull the plug on this." WR

- "I could change the outcome here." TH - "I could hang up my helper cape. I could take off the badge and put down the shield…"

EB - "I could breathe. SE - "I could even relax... just a little." UE - "I could feed my body. UN - "I could let myself go to the bathroom." CH - "I might even let myself get some sleep."

CB - "I might delegate something." UA - "And maybe the delegating would show me," LP - "or teach me that it was easy to ask for help." WR - "But it isn't. I can't!" TH - "But then again. Maybe it is time to have some help."

Go ahead and stretch.

Okay. Where would you like to continue 'poking this bear?'

Participant: I think we poked lots of holes in that one! It is draining. It is moving.

I want to know who I should call. Where do I start?

Kathy: I would start with my team. 'Dear team, you know, I need assistance. I am willing now to have the assistance. Send me the people… Whether it's physically, mentally, emotionally for my support in this process.'

And then pay attention to whomever pops into your mind. You can check in with yourself and clarify before you contact them. Okay? And then you message them and say, 'Hey, this thing is happening in my world right now. Do you happen to know anything about this?'

Sometimes it's them directly. And sometimes it's them referring you to a resource.

197

Keep breathing. Notice how you are feeling and feel for any other threads or waves of emotion- tapping always continues for a bit.

So, you know, I've generally neglected checking in at the beginning and assessing my level of discomfort before I start tapping. I just tap a little and move on with my day.

But the idea of having notes is on paper, as you write down your topics and how big the SUDS level is out of 10. Then after you've done a couple rounds of tapping. And maybe if you daisy-chain and hit other topics, you write down those aspects too. Then when you come back to see your own entries, maybe dropping an 8 to a 5, you can celebrate the contrast. But also see about taking that residual 5 down further.

And then a couple days a week, maybe a month later, you'd look at it again. And go 'Really? Oh, yeah. I remember when it was that high for me.'

We are energetic beings, and you are addressing the energy of your meridian pathways as you tap on the acupoints. You're asking things to move; asking your body to clear and reset.

Whenever you do that there's a ripple effect. And so, it will continue toppling other quiet or hidden aspects until it gets to something that's pretty solid, and the wave of electrical soothing can't just resolve it behind the scenes for you. But that comes to your awareness. You might 'be triggered about something.' Then that's your next topic.

Other times we will have temperature fluctuations as the circuitry recalibrates. It could be a wave of

198

exhaustion and feeling a need to go lay down. Other days it happens as an influx of vitality, and I feel the desire to go run around.

But all of those are something you might tap for.

Go ahead and tap EB - "I can't think about this." SE - "What's going on right now," UE - "that I'd rather go to sleep than look at this issue?" UN - "There's something here." CH - "I really don't want to know something."

CB - "Why do I NOT want to know it?" UA - "Did I make a promise at some point?" LP - "Did I abdicate my authority on that topic at some point?" WR - "Now I can't go there at all." And also, TH - "Oh my gosh! I have a million things to do. I NEED to jump up and run away so I don't look at what this is and feel something I'm avoiding!"

Okay? Ask yourself, 'what's going on with me?' 'What is this? 'What's the significance of this topic/ issue/event?' or 'What was happening 30 seconds before I went on that shopping spree?'

Another version of that kind of avoidance is going to eat something. There are a lot of people who do emotional eating; they weren't really craving anything. But there is something in their thoughts or experience, about to come up, emotionally or mentally and they pop over to 'Oh, I've gotta go eat something! I need salty or crunchy or I need sweet!' ASAP.

Participant: I never thought about it like that. That wanting candy had anything to do with what I was thinking about.

Kathy: Yes, sweet is a great big one. Let's go ahead and actually do a round for sweet and financial together.

Rub the sore spot or tap the side of the hand.

KC - "Even though any amount of money can be bitter, and money can be sweet like candy, I love who I am. I love that I have experienced some sweetness with money! And I have experienced a whole lot of bitterness. Right now, I embrace and honor who I am and all of my experiences. Especially because I have been through the sweet and the bitter times with money."

EB - "Money can be so sweet!" SE - "Sweet money." UE - "It buys wonderful things." UN – " I've had amazing experiences with money to provide the sweetness of life." CH - "I have also seen sour, bitterness and gall with money."

CB - "With the lack of money and debt that crushes us." UA - "Sometimes I desire money. I taste it in my mouth." LP - "I taste the sweetness of what it would be like to have money come to me with ease." WR - "Sometimes I know there isn't enough. I expect emptiness." TH - "And I taste in my mouth like ashes and blackness." Deep breath.

EB - "Money can be sweet." SE - "Most of the time I'm disappointed." UE - "I'm misaligned." UN - "Money shows up, but it's not what I thought it was." CH - "It's not enough."

CB - "The money doesn't last the way I wanted it to." UA - "And I crave the sweetness and fullness." LP - "I want my money to be sweet and sufficient for my needs." WR - "I'm so sorry and even ashamed for the bitterness that that is in my life." TH - "I want the sweetness so much!" Deep breath.

EB - "Sometimes I pretend things are good." SE - "I use my money to buy a sweet substitute." UE - "Candies, chocolates." UN - "Luxurious desserts." CH - "I purchase for the momentary experience."

CB - "Eating sweetness, as though tasting it will fulfill that need." UA - "It is fleeting, momentary joy." LP - "And then later, bitterness again." WR - "Empty wrappers and empty feelings." TH - "I have regret for the sweetness that I pretended to have and the contrast that it highlighted in my lack." Take a deep breath.

EB - "All those places where I chose quick, fleeting sweetness." SE - "and I traded it… I robbed myself of the long-term sweetness…." Deep breath. UE - "I live in a world that pushes me to speed." UN - "I live in a world so full of bitterness." CH - "There is so much grief and unmanageable sorrow."

CB - "I have some money. I can spend it on sugar and feel okay for a moment. "UA - "Most of the time. I don't believe that there's any long-term impact." LP - "I could choose to have candy, or not, and it doesn't matter." WR - "I can go overboard and make myself sick by binging on sugar. But that doesn't help me." TH - "I've been told. I've been taught that joy is fleeting, and bitterness is lasting."

EB - "I have collapsed these things with money." SE - "These things are not what money is." UE - "My community, my culture is addicted to sugar." UN - "I have been addicted as a way to avoid uncomfortable things." CH - "It was in my training. It was in my upbringing."

CB - "To reach for the immediate gratification of sugar." UA - "Even if it meant the long-term cost of

201

sacrificing my health." LP - "I see these things and I am weary." WR - "Avoidance and stuffing my emotions with a sugar-coated habit." TH - "It's such a big problem. And there are so many people caught in it with me." Deep breath.

EB - "Seeing this ... saying it is hard." SE - "I really don't like talking about this." UE - "I like my sweets." UN - "I like my sugar." CH - "I'm just being honest..."

CB - "I'd rather not address the bitterness." UA - "All the people around me are living from one sugar rush to the next." LP - "It seems like work to be authentic this way." WR - "I don't want to give up sweetness. I don't want to be left out of the celebrations." TH - "I don't want to deprive myself of sugar or rob myself of those small joys. Why? Because I've forgotten about other choices that bring me sweetness." Deep breath.

EB - "Right now I choose to remember that there are things worth enjoying." SE - "There are other ways, with or without money, to enjoy my reality." UE - "There are choices I can make." UN - "There are actions I can take." CH - "Any day will work. And I can be in any place." Take a deep breath.

CB - "I can ask 'Where's the beauty in this?' and be shown beauty." UA - "Universe? Show me the beauty of who I am." LP - "I'm open to perceiving and receiving the beauty of my life." WR - "I have gratitude for what is working to create my joy right now." TH - "Dear brain, please show me something beautiful each day."

EB - "I choose to appreciate and have gratitude." SE - "I choose to acknowledge the marvelous and beautiful world." UE - " I choose to remember what has gone well for me." UN - "And as I do this with intention, I curate my life." CH - "I change the balance of sweetness and bitterness by where I give my attention."

CB - "I bet the more time I spend in gratitude and in appreciating myself, there will be less need for sugar." UA - "There will be less need for sugar and false joy." LP - "I'm willing to find out what can change in my life." WR - "I'm willing to give my attention to remembering and acknowledging sweet people and sweet experiences." TH - "I'm willing to have authentic and lasting sweetness now."

Sit with that for just a minute.

How are you feeling?

Participant: I'm a lot more relaxed in my body. There's tenderness... I'm feeling soft in my heart right now.

Kathy: Neat. I wonder, what would it take to have more of that in your daily life? I hope you will choose to create that experience.

Questions and Illumination

Try out this question. "What can I be, do, and allow, that would create and generate financial success, now and in the future?" Pause and breathe.

Notice how you feel about being, doing, and allowing. Are you able to create and generate anything? Is financial success something that feels obtainable for you, why or why not?

Asking questions, and pausing to feel what popped up, is one of the primary ways to find the threads of content for rounds of tapping.

The founder of Access Consciousness (not related to EFT) has written several books and taught classes all over the world. One of the fundamental tools I have received from Gary Douglas is the concept of 'being in the question' of life.

Furthermore, the teachings from Access Consciousness encourage everyone to hold information gently and leave room for the energy to shift. Asking a question is not about getting the right answer, but it is a way to gain awareness.

Gary M. Douglas said, "We have a choice in life. We can choose to live by other people's realities and the limited menu that has been handed to us, or we can choose something different.

We can choose to be walled in by normalcy, consistency, and judgment, or we can choose to create our own reality.

If this reality isn't working for you, realize that you have a different possibility available."

I find that I agree with his sentiment. I know that the changes I desire for my life are going to come about through my own dedication and as an expression of my ability to adapt what I have been given into something I enjoy.

I've been asking, "Where is the convergence of my creation with the desire of a generative universe to be joyfully expressed through me and flowing with the dance of prosperity?"

A long time ago I learned that in Sanskrit the word 'Human' means 'The dispenser of Divine Gifts.' I really love that definition. It feels like a reality I'd like to live in.

Ok. Let's talk about closing the gap between where you feel that you are and where you would like to be with your life.

Setting a goal will always produce the illusion of a gap in our minds. It is an interesting challenge to work towards an outcome but not plant it in your mind as something that you are telling yourself you do not or cannot have.

It can be fun to tap with intentionally collapsed timelines... To say, 'I envision this.' and then speak of your life as having that fully accomplished.

When we Future pace our dialog the discrepancy of feeling it is lacking will automatically come up to be resolved. Then, if you tap through the acupoints as you talk it can be released at the same time.

We are always consistent with the way we think about ourselves. You can look to your current outcomes to see the evidence of how you have been thinking.

You may like this version of tapping and want to do a lot more… and you may hate it for the cognitive dissonance it kicks up.

Let's give it a try. I'd like you all to get into the habit of thinking about yourselves this way.

EB - "I am a being of light! I am a truth-seeker!" SE - "I am an expert!" UE - "I am successful." UN - "I am awesome!" CH - "I am here to experience many wonderful things, including ease with money."

CB - "I bring clarity and inspiration!" UA - "I am attuned to the frequencies of financial success." LP - "I resonate with financial wealth." WR - "Everything works for me. I receive and maintain prosperity." TH - "I accept the Divine imprint of money and miracles."

EB - "I have loving acceptance for who I am and all of my journey." SE - "I embrace and accept abundant wealth." UE - "I am provided for in miraculous and mundane ways." UN - "My needs are met, and I am prosperous." CH - "I am grateful, and I am loved." Deep breath.

CB - "I know that I am Love." UA - "I know that I am Light." LP - "I know that I am Infinite." WR - "I know that I am capable of amazing things." and, the mantra of Access Consciousness at the TH - "All of life comes to me with ease, joy and glory."

Blink, blink, blink. Look around the room. Stretch. Move around some. Breathe. Maybe get some water.

The same way we get deep and dark shadows right next to a bright flood light; tapping with just positive, present tense affirmations will accentuate and make any negative self-talk in your mind feel very loud.

So, whatever those bullying thoughts were, notice and be sure to keep tapping a few rounds to dissolve those negative root statements.

Then when you come back to more bright and positive self-affirmations you will get to receive and integrate them on new levels.

When you can step into your congruent and authentic nature your ability to harmonize with the universe is amplified and many people will be happy to pay you for your skills and services.

Participant: I'm still not sure about what my success would be... I mean, I don't have a business or independent company and I don't know that I want to build that way to get to my financial success.

Kathy: That's perfectly fine. All the clearings and tools that work for someone running a business will also work for an individual. I'm sure you've heard, 'We are all in the business of living.

It is good to check in with our hesitations and doubts. Questions like 'Am I completely ready to have this in my life?', 'Who will I have to be when my life works this way?' and 'How does it get easier than this?' will bring up very valuable perspectives about the pros and cons of following a particular path forward.

Mental noise. The 'monkey mind' chatter can show you the backlash from your inner critic and saboteur.

Learn to hear it clearly. See it, acknowledge it for playing those old program tapes. Speak it out loud and tap through the acupoints so that your body can remap the circuitry of clarity at the same time you are exposing those lies to the light of scrutiny.

Know that many of these harsh things are rooted in fear and have been maintained because there was not a better option. They were installed to protect you and keep you from anticipated pain when you did not have other tools.

That is different now.

The aspects of wounded inner self that were committed to keeping you safe through hesitation, guilt, shame, doubt, anxiety, and fear can be released from that burden.

Your commitment to yourself can clear, release, resolve, dissolve, destroy and uncreate all the lies and twisted stupidities of your past.

Emotional Freedom Techniques, applied regularly and liberally, can bring you the space for healing and restoration of your wholeness.

I look forward to hearing all about your success and I will gladly join you in celebration of your new life.

Never Enough

Let's clear away some of the blocks to have ease with your money flows!

Ready? Take a deep breath. Sit and think about the amount of money you are earning right now. Notice if that creates some feelings in you. Close your eyes for a minute.

Now state out loud, "It's not enough." If that feels true for you, what is your SUDS level?

KC - "Even though I am distressed about the amount of money in my life, I deeply and completely love and accept myself. I am concerned about my money and right now I choose to love and accept myself. I approve of who I am even though I do not have enough money coming to me right now."

EB - "I don't think that there is enough money for me." SE - "I try to get by with what money I have," UE - "but it never seems to be enough for the demands of my life." UN - "Even though it is just not enough money," CH - "I honor my feelings and choose to acknowledge what I am thinking."

CB - "There's more month at the end of the money." UA - "I'm feeling ashamed and afraid." LP - "I'm feeling worried and confused." WR - "What if I can't change this? What if I'm doomed to failure?" TH - "What if my money reality never improves?"

EB - "I don't have enough money in my account." SE - "There isn't enough money to buy groceries." UE -

"There isn't enough money to buy clothing and shoes." UN - "There isn't enough money to pay the bills." CH - "I am afraid money won't ever be enough for me."

CB - "When I think about my money and the low number in my account, I feel sad, and afraid." UA - "It's easy to be angry or depressed about things; it is just not enough money." LP - "I've been wrestling with these low numbers," WR - "and these low feelings for a long time." TH - "Something needs to change about the money in my life. I am willing for things to be different with my money." Deep breath

Check in with your SUDS level. If it is still high or has not moved, you may need to revisit the Gamut Point Technique that was shared at the beginning of this book for correcting polarity reversal.

Let's keep going.

EB - "I've been maintaining that my money is never enough for me." SE - "I get scared, and I get angry when I see how little money there is." UE - "It isn't enough!" UN - "I say it is the money that failed me." CH - "Or maybe I blame someone for pinching off the money that should be flowing to my account." Deep breath.

CB - "I am willing for this to shift. I am open to having new experiences with money." UA - "I could be mad at myself. I might be afraid that I am not enough." LP - "I might be blaming myself for the financial shortfall." WR - "It's miserable to think that I am not enough or that I can't figure out my finances." TH - "Self-loathing and financial hardship go hand in hand. This totally sucks."

EB - "And here I am tapping… again…still." SE - "Something must be changing for me to be here and using this process." UE - "This frustration is just another aspect of the conglomerate financial inheritance I am unraveling." UN - "I am making progress." CH - "I am feeling better more often."

CB - "I am willing to believe that I can feel even better about myself and my money." UA - "I may not yet have evidence of change in the world, but I can make changes in myself." LP - "There's a bunch I cannot control. I know that." WR - "I'm seeing now that I can sway my own thoughts and shape my inner landscape." TH - "Even though my income still isn't enough, I am open to change my thoughts and feelings about money." Deep breath.

EB - "I am not sure how my money reality will change." SE - "I am not sure when my money reality will change." UE - "I don't know who can help me adjust my money reality in healthy ways." UN - "I do know that I am willing to adapt and reset." CH - "I am available for graceful changes with my finances."

CB - "I make myself available for change." UA - "I am even willing to change my opinions about myself to change my relationship with money." LP - "I am available for healthy and legal forms of income." WR - "I am open to receive money that provides for my body and my family with gentle kindness." TH - "I'm even willing to have all of life come to me with ease, joy and glory."

Pause. Breathe. Check your SUDS level and make notes about this topic of 'Money is not enough.' Vs. 'I am not enough.'

You will likely need to revisit this area a few times to find the bits of relevant information that your system needs to release.

Remember to include tapping for the positive and fluffy content when you feel the space open up.

It's a bit like nourishing your physical body with vitamins and minerals; the affirmations and praise strengthen your sense of self and rebuild your emotional body.

This is an ongoing system for sustaining your life, not an all at once, one-and-done kind of tactic.

Achieving Financial Targets

We will be tapping today around the energy of meeting financial goals. Notice what doubts or old memories come up and if you have a SUDS level about either failing to meet a target or reaching completion.

Either rub the sore spot in circles or start on the side of the hand.

KC - "Even though I have not met my current financial goals, I deeply and completely love and accept myself. Even though I'm not making as much money as I would like to make, I choose now to lovingly accept all of me." Still on the side of the hand "My financial goals are not working as easily as I would like to have them work… And I deeply and completely love and accept myself."

EB - "There's a financial target that I have in mind." SE - "There's a number and I haven't gotten there yet." UE - "I have all sorts of reasons why I think, and I believe, that that much money would be better than what I have right now." UN - "I keep pushing myself to change. I keep pushing myself to do better." CH - "When I finally earn that much money, my life will change." Deep breath.

CB - "I have all these ideas, all these plans for what I can do and who I can be later." UA - "My financial targets are way out there." LP - "In fact, my financial targets keep moving." WR - "I am dissatisfied with my financial progress partially because I keep striving for better." TH - "I think it's good that I am aspiring to have more, to achieve bigger, to be better."

EB - "And in all of this, I have not been very patient with myself." SE - "My money targets are a way that I

213

drive myself to keep working harder." UE - "I drive myself to keep putting in more hours." Deep breath. UN - "I have these financial targets." CH – "I have these ideas that when I earn a certain amount of money, I will finally be able to rest." Deep breath.

CB - "I will finally be able to play and be able to enjoy my life." UA - "I keep putting off some of the things I would like to do because I haven't made enough money yet." LP - "In fact, part of this is because I want to prove something to myself or prove something to someone else about money." WR – "I have attached a lot of significance to these projections, these expectations and financial targets" TH - "I have attached emotional need and validation to my income goals."

EB - "There has been so much significance around making money." SE - "There's so much significance about missing my targets." UE - "So much emotional content wrapped up in the amount of my income." UN - "I've made my income mean something about who I am." CH - "That's a lot of stress." Deep breath.

CB - "These places where I've twisted financial success into emotional well-being." UA - "I've made financial income mean something about who I am." LP - "I've made a lack of financial income mean that something is wrong with me." WR - "I think when I finally make a certain amount of money, then I'll be successful." TH - "I've made it mean that if I have that much income, I can be happy being who I am."

EB - "I've been delaying my life in search of how to make money." SE - "I've been avoiding my life seeking income." UE - "That's kind of silly and very uncomfortable.". UN - " I can see how that doesn't really work." CH - " I've been putting off enjoying my life trying to be good enough, worthy or valid." Deep breath.

CB - "It doesn't really make sense, trying to be something for the sake of income. That is not true to my inner nature." UA - "What's the use of having a lot of money, if I'm not enjoying who I am, or how my life is going?" LP - "This pattern is convoluted and frustrating." WR - "I know I've duplicated this bastardization from the world around me." TH - "I can see that. Maybe there's room for another layer of release, rebalancing, and recalibration." Deep breath.

EB - "I could have more balance in the creation and the generation of my finances." SE - "I could allow for necessary income and the enjoyment of my life along the way." UE - "In fact, I could have a lot more fun and joy with making and having money." UN - "I wonder what that looks like." CH - "I wonder what that feels like to have more fun making an income." Deep breath.

CB - "I am willing to find out how I can have a lot more fun and have consistent income at the same time." UA - "I wonder how my body would like to participate in growing my business." LP - "I wonder how my business would like to generate more fun and joy with me as we grow together?" WR - "And I am curious, how will my financial success impact the people around me?" TH - "I look forward to finding out how much easier reaching my financial targets can actually be. I choose to work with my body and with my business."

EB - "Making money. Receiving payments and having money could be awesome fun." SE - "No. There are too many ways to spend money faster than it comes in." UE - "I'm willing to know that there are also a lot of ways to have income and grow my resources." UN - "Having more savings; having a greater income could mean that there has been a greater exchange of my products and services in the world." CH - "I get to express my brilliance and be compensated."

CB - "That would be so great. I would like to have the world benefiting more from my gifts and capacities!" UA - "I choose now to be positive in my vision for the future." LP - "I choose now to be spacious with anything that feels joyful." WR - "I can see I've been pulling myself to enjoy my life and to create a financial future I will love to live." TH - "I know that many things are possible now as I embrace more of who I am." Deep breath.

EB - "I know that by having more fun I raise my overall vibrations." SE - "That is actually a contribution to my health and all the people around me too." UE - "I do have a lot that I wish to accomplish." UN - "I am also willing to benefit as the people around me shift their frequencies." CH - "I am willing now to soften, relax and to receive goodness and kindness with money." Deep breath.

CB - "I choose to focus on the benefits of my success. I choose to notice and acknowledge where I am making progress." UA - "I have made so much progress with my financial reality." LP - "I choose to celebrate my progress." WR - "I love all that I have accomplished." TH - "I'm so glad that I am choosing to change my money and open space for new financial outcomes in my life." Deep breath.

Check in. Do you have loose ends to address?

Was there much negative mind chatter that came up as we went to positive statements? What's your current SUDS level about your ability to achieve a financial target? What about the SUDS level in anticipation of missing a target?

Would your system benefit from more tapping on one or more of those positive statements? Do you need to back up and do other EFT rounds for an old wound?

Authentic Vulnerability

KC - "Opening space feels unfamiliar, and I love myself anyway. I'm not entirely sure how to open space for receiving but right now, I love and accept who I am. I love who I am even when I need more space to relax and allow money to show up in my life."

EB - "When I have ease, joy and glory with receiving money, then I will be able to relax!" SE - "Then it will be time to slow down and breathe." UE - "I will finally be validated in the work that I do when money is flowing easily." UN - "I will prove that I really do offer value!" CH - "I'll know that I have succeeded because I will be wealthy."

CB - "I'll have lots of money and everyone will know that I am successful!" UA – "I've attached my sense of self-worth to my income goals." LP - "I know that that doesn't make sense." WR - "I know that I overreact because I have been unwilling to acknowledge my own disappointment and grief around money." TH - "All that that is, I unbind, uninstall, destroy and uncreate it."

EB - "I know that I've been reacting and living from old financial wounds." SE - "I've been living from lies and anticipating financial hardship." UE - "I've been using those old patterns to keep myself stuck." UN - "There is not actually any obligation to carry on struggling just because I have struggled in the past!" CH - "I choose to remember that I am an infinite being." Deep breath.

CB - "I've done a lot of work to acknowledge and release the pain of my financial past." UA - "I have learned a lot about who I used to be, and why I set my life up to run with financially dysfunctional autopilots." LP - "My old

218

patterns did serve to keep me functioning within the established loop of perceived safety." WR - "I now destroy and uncreate everything in the way of my integration, my joy and success with money." TH - "I know now that 'safety' can be arbitrary and it is something that I get to choose to create for myself and maintain for my own physiology."

EB - "When I allow money to be with me in a peaceful way, it is easy and graceful for me to be more of myself." SE - "I am able to play and have fun." UE - "I am free to rest and rejuvenate." UN - "Everything that has kept this bound up within me, as an inaccessible or imaginary story..." CH - "That I can't play ... That I can't relax."

CB - "That I can't have fun until after the money is made" UA - "And I can't be myself until after the bills are paid." LP - "I destroy and uncreate it now." WR - "Across all time, space, dimensions and realities, known and unknown." TH - "I call my power back to myself. I reclaim my own authority within myself and my body to build and maintain my wealth and success with the speed of grace."

EB - "Having lots of money can be fun!" SE - "There are so many ways to joyfully expend and invest it." UE - "I am willing now to allow myself to enjoy the play of money." UN - "More income means that more people are enjoying my products and services." CH - "I am being seen, appreciated and valued by others and within myself."

CB - "I get to give the gift of who I am in vibrant and dynamic ways." UA - "I choose to be positive and spacious with all of this." LP - "I give permission for the residue of old pain, hesitation or doubt to exit my body in gentle and efficient ways." WR - "I know that I am Love. I know that I am light." TH - "I know that I am infinite and infinitely capable of shifting and changing my reality." Deep breath.

EB - "I choose to soften, to relax and to lower my barriers." SE - "I choose to receive my own well-being from the deep well of my soul." UE - "I choose to remember, from within myself, all that I am." UN - "I choose to focus on my progress and my success." CH - "I choose for my net income from all channels to increase monthly." Deep breath.

CB - "I enjoy quality time and healthy relationships with my friends and family." UA - "I open the space and invite financial abundance to find me." LP - "I welcome financial prosperity and I choose to live in balanced ways." WR - "I choose my professional status." TH - "I open space to be respected, paid and sought after for my skills and abilities."

EB - "I choose to live in a beautiful home." SE - "One that easily accommodates the needs, desires and hobbies of my whole family." UE - "I choose to love myself." UN - "I choose to be loved and loving." CH - "I take charge of my life and create it as abundant and sustainable." Deep breath.

CB - "I value and respect my physical, mental, emotional and spiritual health as I grow with my wealth and financial resources." UA - "I have freedom to create in each circumstance." LP - "I choose to be true to myself." WR - "I have internal congruence, kindness, peace and joy while I have growing income." TH - "I know that All of Life comes to me with ease, joy and glory as I am a Great and Glorious Creator."

Pause. Notice. Breathe and stretch.

Do you need more tapping, or integration time right now?

The Flow of Creation vs. Fear

There is often a lot of heaviness and resistance around this topic. We will be spending a few more rounds going through the unhappy thoughts to give voice and space for those feelings to be addressed with the tapping before moving into the positive affirmations again.

Especially if this is uncomfortable, please keep tapping through the disquiet of your mental chatter.

Don't leave off in the middle of a dark thought and let yourself fester in despair, regret, or grief. Those are tappable issues. Get assistance if you need help making it through [ANY] aspects of this material.

We're going to start on the side of the hand. Remember to tap gently and speak these statements and questions out loud so that your body and mind can hear you voice these things at the same time the meridians are being cleared and reset.

KC - "Even though I don't feel that I am aligned I deeply and completely love and accept myself. Even though aligning with the flow seems to be difficult I choose now to love and embrace all aspects of myself. Aligning with the flow has been difficult and I love all of myself."

EB - "I can't have what I want." SE - "I'm not even on my side." UE - "I don't feel like anyone is on my side." UN - "I feel guilty when I get what I want." CH - "I will always find a way to mess up my success."

CB - "I'm not allowed to have more than others!" UA - "My success hurts people." LP - "I worry that my progress is painful for others." WR - "What if my having what I want would hurt someone else?" TH - "I can't have what I want and make sure everyone else is fine too." Deep breath.

EB - "I'm confused. I avoid being whole." SE - "I don't trust the Source of all that is." UE - "I don't trust people to help me." UN - "I feel like the world is out to get me." CH - "In fact I think I know the world is out to get me!"

CB - "I've been experiencing that the world is out to get me." UA - "I don't belong here." LP - "People don't like me or want me to succeed." WR - "There's always something that goes wrong at some point." TH - "And I am afraid that I am inadequate for the task ahead of me." Deep breath.

EB - "I am afraid I will misuse or abuse power if I have it." SE - "I don't know what actions are important for me to take." UE - "I don't know what actions I need to discard or avoid." UN - "I don't have the energy to manifest my potential!" CH - "I can't have what I want."

CB - "How could I have what I want?" UA - "I'm not on my side." LP - "I will feel guilty if I get what I want." WR - "There are good reasons for me to fail… again." TH - "I'm really good at messing things up. Hoping is hard work." Deep breath.

EB - "I will always find a way to mess up my progress." SE - "I am too loud and disorganized." UE - "my success hurts other people somehow." UN - "I don't trust myself to accurately navigate my challenges." CH - "I don't trust myself to do what needs doing in a timely manner."

CB - "I don't trust Source to lead or direct me." UA - "I don't trust people to be good to me." LP - "I am hesitant and too quiet to do well." WR - "I am suspicious of the world around me." TH - "I don't belong here! Of course, things can't go well for me." Deep breath.

EB - "I'm afraid. I am inadequate." SE - "I'm afraid that if I succeed, I will misuse or abuse my power." UE - "I don't know what actions are important." UN - "I don't know what actions to discard and ignore." CH - "I don't have energy to manifest my potential and actualize my dreams." Deep breath.

CB - "I don't think I can achieve my best." UA - "The freedom to play is for other people to enjoy." LP - "I can't just play AND make progress." WR - "I'm overwhelmed and exhausted just thinking about it." TH - "This is all so serious and daunting." Deep breath.

EB - "I would like to see the Divine in every aspect of creation." SE - "I would like to accept what is and go into inspired action." UE - "I would like to proceed... to persevere and reach success." UN - "Giving up on my dreams does seem easier." CH - "I'm tired and I've burned through a lot of resources already." Long, slow, deep breath. Follow it in and out.

CB - "I think I can't have what I want." UA - "I'm not on my side." LP - "I've been thinking that I can't win for a long time." WR - "I've been carrying the burden of self-defeat in my mind." TH - "I'm not allowed to have more than others. It wouldn't be right for me to succeed when so many people are failing."

EB - "And I suspect that my success somehow hurts people." SE - "Obviously I'm going to avoid being whole and achieving my success!" UE - "I'm not willing to receive my prize with so many doubts and concerns." UN -

"I don't trust people to actually support me or to celebrate my success if I have it." CH - "I'd like to trust people… It would be nice to have people to trust." Deep breath.

CB - "The world is out to get me though." UA - "I just don't belong here." LP - "I've been told that it's a 'dog-eat-dog' kind of place." WR - "Isn't everything set up to support 'survival of the fittest' or something?" TH - "I'm afraid I'll step forward and crash into expensive or catastrophic failure!"

Deep breath. Keep breathing as we work through this material.

EB - "I just know I'm going to mess it up." SE - "What's the point if I persevere and reach success but then can't keep it?" UE - "I'm afraid I will misuse or abuse my power." UN - "Because I don't know which actions are inspired." CH - "And I don't know which people to trust."

CB - "I don't even trust myself." UA - "I don't trust my Source LP - "I feel alone here." WR - "I feel cheated and abandoned." TH - "Why would I look for the Divine in every aspect of creation?" Deep breath.

EB - "Why would I persevere?" SE - "I'm really good at feeling guilty and ashamed." UE - "I'm very good at stopping myself." UN - "I'm really good at avoiding success." CH - "I'm not willing to receive change unless I can micromanage it."

CB - "I'm not willing to trust or hope for change." UA - "I don't want to persevere and work towards my targets." LP - "I can't have it anyway." WR - "I wouldn't be able to keep it if I got it." TH - "Aligning with the flow is hard work!" Deep breath. Good work moving through all of that 'stirring up the muck.'

We are shifting gears a little here.

EB - "What if I could have what I want?" SE - "What if I could be on my side no matter what?" UE - "What if I don't have to feel guilty for getting what I want?" UN - "What if guilt is a lie and shame is a distraction?" CH - "If I can find a way to mess things up, somewhere that might mean *I do* have an awareness of what would work."

CB - "What if I could have everything I desire?" UA - "I might be allowed to have more even if other people do not choose to have more." LP - "Maybe I live on a planet with ridiculous levels of abundance?" WR - "I might be able to have my needs met from the surplus of available wealth on this planet." TH - "I could choose to have more than I used to have. What if I raise my own set points and find new ways to receive with grace?"

EB - "Even if others do not choose to have what I choose to have." SE - "I could have more from the space of 'out creating' my own past." UE - "I could align with the flow sometimes and see how it goes." UN - "I could avoid being in alignment and that doesn't suddenly make other people have what they are missing." CH - "My success or failure could be independent of anyone else's success or failure."

CB - "My experience of my reality is happening inside of me." UA - "My failure or success won't automatically change what other people are choosing." LP - "I know I'm not in charge of what happens for other people." WR - "There is a lot going on in each moment of each day." TH - "I can't know everything about everyone. I could trust myself sometimes. I could lean into this idea of trusting Source."

EB - "I could let myself choose 'wholeness' as a target." SE - "I could be willing to receive inspiration." UE - "Blocking receiving could mean that *I do* know how to receive." UN - "I could trust people to help me when they are trustworthy people." CH - "I could trust the world to be complex and changeable."

CB - "I could start to belong here." UA - "I might be able to choose what that means to me." LP - "I can shape the nature of how I fit with a team or community of people." WR - "I was in a habitual pattern of isolation and fear." TH - "Habits can be changed. I was afraid. I do not have to stay afraid." Deep breath.

EB - "I held myself as inadequate in my own mind." SE - "Maybe 'afraid' and 'inadequate' are lies I've been telling myself to fit in." UE - "Maybe. It could be that I am aware of everyone else's fear and self-doubt too." UN - "Maybe I perceive where they feel inadequate?" CH - "I might perceive where they are afraid that there will be an abuse of power, from anyone."

CB - "What if I could trust myself?" UA - "It might be okay to have power and potency with inspiration." LP - "I still don't think I know what actions are important." WR - "Maybe that's okay, to go slow and not know everything right now." TH - "I could have energy to grow. I could achieve my best gradually."

EB - "I can be open to play spontaneously." SE - "I have been witnessing other people play." UE - "All that that is, everywhere I've been resisting playfulness with

227

money." UN - "Maybe part of that is knowing how?" CH - "I have to know what it is to resist it." Deep breath.

CB - "I could be open to trusting myself." UA - "Maybe playfulness is not something that I will schedule." LP - "Perhaps playfulness and inspiration have a lot in common." WR - "Maybe being unwilling to play has contributed to my lack of inspiration." TH - "I open space for the energy of play and the energy of inspiration to grow in my life and with my money too." Deep breath.

EB - "I can have what I choose to create with my money and my life." SE - "I am on my side. I have my vote of confidence." UE - "I think of myself as capable." UN - "Carrying fear, guilt and self-doubt was a habit. Now I have a choice about keeping them" CH - "I can feel how I would like to feel and take inspired actions with my money."

CB - "I am not obligated to mess up or fail." UA - "I could have more money and resources than other people will choose to allow." LP - "I can participate with flows of abundance." WR - "There are frequencies and opportunities available to me that I used to block out." TH - "Some people might think I'm too much.... of something."

EB - "Some people might say I'm going 'too fast' or 'too slow'." SE - "Someone might think I'm choosing 'too much' or 'not enough'." UE - "There are people who might think that my success hurts them in some way." UN - "They may choose to be disempowered by my success or my failure!" CH - "I have that choice too. I could be disempowered by my success or failure." Deep breath.

CB - "I could be disempowered by anyone's success or failure." UA - "It's a choice. I choose the way I will think about myself." LP - "I choose to cultivate positive and uplifting messages in my mind." WR - "I get to curate my inner world and cascade those thoughts into new habits and behaviors." TH - "I choose to choose my financial success."

EB - "I choose to be respectful and kind when I speak of myself." SE - "I choose to honor and trust myself." UE - "I choose to trust people who show themselves to be trustworthy." UN - "I choose to know that I belong here in many ways."

CB - "I choose to know that I am suited for the challenges of my life." UA - "I choose to trust myself with power." LP - "I claim my capacities and my potency." WR - "I know that my growth will be ongoing, and I trust myself to adapt to the changing world." TH - "I choose to know what actions are important to take and when to step back."

EB - "I choose to know what actions need to be discontinued." SE - "I choose to use my energy to generate and actualize my financial success." UE - "I choose to achieve my best each day." UN - "I will play spontaneously." CH - "I am willing to see the Divine in every aspect of creation." Deep breath.

CB - "I accept what is and what was." UA - "I am committed to achieving my success." LP - "Success is a variable target." WR - "I get to define how my success looks and how it feels." TH - "My success is an ongoing choice." Deep breath.

EB - "I have success." SE - "I enjoy my progress." UE - "I enjoy my success." UN - "I do enjoy my success in many ways." CH - "Success can be playful and joyful."

CB - "I could have a lot of fun with financial success." UA - "The amount of fun I have each day is up to me." LP - "I joyfully take inspired actions." WR - "I have bright ideas and follow through with actionable steps." TH - "I get to play with inspiration and have fun achieving my best outcomes." Deep breath.

EB - "Being spontaneously playful." SE - "Playing with success." UE - "The Divine could support and inspire me." UN - "I could feel supported in each circumstance of each day." CH - "Aligning with the flow of creation could be easy and fun?!"

CB - "I'm willing to have play become my alignment." UA - "Maybe when I play, I am aligned." LP - "Maybe alignment is playful?" WR - "I could playfully align myself with inspiration." TH - "All of that, where I've been aware of everyone else resisting the flow… I can know what is and is not mine." Deep breath.

EB - "I can have miraculous and mundane outcomes." SE - "What if I am who I am, and things work for me?" UE - "I trust myself and Divinity." UN - "I trust my success to grow as I grow." CH - "I trust the world to flow around me and change as I change."

CB - "I belong to myself, and I am guided." UA - "I know what actions to take to generate desired outcomes." LP - "I am one of those Divinely guided and inspired people." WR - "My life works in miraculous and mundane ways as I participate with the flows of creation." TH - "I have more than enough. I am more than enough."

EB - "I achieve my best." SE - "My best is more than good enough." UE - " I am right where I desire to be."

UN - "I am right for my life." CH - "I see the Divine in every aspect of creation and in my life."

CB - "I see the Divine within myself." UA - "I persevere to reach my targets and I am happy to succeed." LP - "I create beyond my old hesitations and limitations." WR - "I exceed my old ways of thinking and dream bigger dreams." TH - "Sustainable success is available for me to enjoy." Deep breath.

EB - "All of this stuff about money... it's not all mine." SE - "And that's okay." UE - "I am so aware of the people around me." UN - "My awareness is a capacity that I have." CH - "I can use my awareness to take care of myself in new ways."

CB - "I can choose to trust my capacities." UA - "I can know when to trust the people around me." LP - "I can know when to walk away from invitations." WR - "My awareness can bless my life." TH - "Divinity can speak to me through my awareness." Take a breath.

EB - "I belong." SE - "I am safe." UE - " I am successful." UN - "I trust who I am." CH - "I trust."

CB - "The world supports me." UA - "I am powerful." LP - "I am capable." WR - "I am guided." TH - "I am creative."

EB - "I am resourceful. SE - "I know what actions to take." UE - " I trust myself." UN - "I am whole." CH - "I am welcome here."

CB - "In fact, I belong here." UA - "This is my home." LP - "I get to create my financial reality." WR - "I get to play with the dance of creation." TH - "I get to have my home and my life the way I choose to make them."

EB - "This is all my choice. SE - " I can have what works for me." UE - "I'm allowed to change my mind." UN - "I'm allowed to change whatever I would like to change." CH - "My life is mine."

CB - "I trust myself to take care of my finances." UA - "I am connected to inspiration." LP - "I trust myself to take inspired actions." WR - "I have permission to have fun with my financial freedom." TH - "Thank you body for this amazing change in our reality."

Thank you for your tenacity and dedication.

Here again, as always, I'm going to invite you to breathe. Stretch, reassess your discomfort and maybe keep tapping.

I invite you to remember EFT as a tool to help you with whatever's going on wherever you are.

Even if you don't remember to tap in the moment of something... When you do remember, "Oh! I should have been tapping!" you can tap for that you forgot to tap!

And yes, it'll get to be more and more normal and natural for you to regularly utilize this tool and really curate your life.

I hope that you will take your time and choose to work through your emotions and memories gently.

It is up to you. Will you choose to reduce all of your SUDS levels and continue this process of tapping into your financial freedom?

Giving yourself the gift of a long-term commitment with EFT means that you will have a core level change that is stable and sustainable for you as a whole and integrated being capable of choosing your financial success.

I appreciate your commitment to healing and your dedication to growth.

May the progress that you create in your financial reality become a legacy that will ripple change out to joyfully impact the world.

Your guide and EFT facilitator, Katherine Hacking

About Katherine Hacking

Originally from Colorado Springs, Co. Katherine moved several times across the US before going to H.S. in Chevy Chase, MD and attending Brigham Young University as a ceramic arts major in Provo, Utah. She discovered talent in the healing arts after suffering car accident injuries in 2002. Katherine then joyfully studied energy work and began to teach her own classes, as a Universal Life Church Minister, in 2005.

Katherine began as someone seeking her own physical recovery. Twenty years later, she is now an Angel Oracle, Licensed Massage Therapist, Advanced Healing Practitioner with Emotional Freedom Techniques, Reiki, Theta Healing, Quantum Touch ®, Neuro-Linguistic Programming, Touch for Health, the Shekinah Seals, Energetic Facelift, ESSE, Symphony of Possibilities, Access Bars™ and also a teacher for several of those modalities.

Katherine loves to unwrap the possibilities for wholeness and transformation. She works to facilitate open-hearted embodiment, inner alignment, and physical restoration.
She is a mother of 3, artist, teacher & miracle worker.

Learn more at KathyHacking.com

234